T0108251

Printed in the USA
CPSIA information can be obtained
at www.ICGtesting.com
JSHW012040140824
68134JS00033B/3171

9 780874 411577

Sayings of the Fathers

פרקי אבות

With a new Collection of Favourite
MORAL SAYINGS OF THE JEWISH
FATHERS, and a Foreword to this
Edition by *Moses Schonfeld*.

✡   ✡   ✡

Published under the Auspices of the
American Chapter, the Religious
Emergency Council of the Chief
Rabbi of the British Empire, in the
year 5705.

Publishers   ℘   ℘

פרקי אבות

Sayings of the Fathers or *Pirke Aboth*,

the Hebrew Text, with a new English Translation and a Commentary by the *Very Rev. Dr. Joseph H. Hertz*, Chief Rabbi of the British Empire,

Behrman House · Inc.

PUBLISHED BY BEHRMAN HOUSE, INC.

COPYRIGHT 1945 BY JOSEPH H. HERTZ

Printed in the United States of America

www.behrmanhouse.com

ISBN 13: 978-0-87441-157-7

Foreword

It is at a turning point in history that this volume makes its appearance. All over the world, the oppressed in bondage so long are at last shattering their bonds. The armies of fascism are being defeated. Yet the war against their insidious ideas must continue if we are to banish evil and intolerance from the face of the earth. And in this war the reaffirmation of the ethical and moral values of the *Pirke Aboth* can be a powerful weapon against the enemy.

In the wisdom of these ethical sayings we can find an excellent source for evolving the basic philosophy of a decent civilization. Couched in simple, stimulating phrases, many of the Hebrew teachings of the *Pirke Aboth* have long since become part of the structure of democratic society. Not only is it now fitting to emphasize the origin of these principles to the world at large, but Jews themselves, in relearning these tenets of their fathers, will be armed with the oldest and strongest ammunition. A sound code for personal behaviour is a sure foundation for international understanding.

The Sayings of the Fathers is a collection which forms a continuous chain, for the Rabbis and scholars in each generation added their interpretations to those of their predecessors. It was faith in the spirit of these traditions that enabled Israel to survive.

Jews in the English speaking world have, in the person of [5] the Very Reverend Dr. Joseph H. Hertz, a great Rabbi and a master of the succinct phrase. Those familiar with his earlier annotations to the Pentateuch will find the Chief Rabbi's latest work in keeping with the lucid scholarship that has gained him deserved recognition. The new reader will discover an author of great literary skill, and a spiritual guide who successfully stimulates interest in the significant human message of Judaism. The teachings of Israel deserve a wide distribution, and by elucidating this fine collection in English, the Chief Rabbi is reaching the largest community of Jews.

Sayings of the Fathers

The author has graciously donated his royalties to the American Chapter, Religious Emergency Council of the Chief Rabbi of Great Britain, to be utilized by the Council in England to continue its religious ministrations to refugees, evacuees and Allied fighting men.

Moses Schonfeld

Honorary Secretary, American Chapter,
Religious Emergency Council of the Chief
Rabbi of the British Empire.

Introduction

"Sayings of the Fathers" is the most widely known of all the sixty-three tractates of the Mishna. It is unique in character. The Mishna is a code of laws governing Jewish life: its subject matter is, therefore, predominantly legal. But this tractate is almost entirely concerned with moral conduct. It consists, for the greater part, of the favourite maxims—being the epitome of their wisdom and experience—of some sixty Rabbis, extending over a period of nearly five hundred years, from 300 B.C.E. to 200 of the common era. It also contains anonymous sayings, and touches upon various historical and folk-lore themes.

Aboth is the name by which the tractate was originally designated. It means "Fathers," *i.e.* the spiritual patriarchs who preserved and developed the Torah as the living tradition of Israel's Faith. In its opening portion, Aboth gives a "chain" of these teachers and a notable saying of each one. *Sayings of the Fathers* is an appropriate English title, as the work preserves and transmits these winged words of wisdom and piety. It is preferable to the current name, "Ethics of the Fathers," seeing that Aboth is not a systematic ethical treatise. The wisdom of the sages in every people finds its way to the masses, by means only of the proverb, saying, or parable. So was it also in Israel. These moral and religious aphorisms came also to be known as *Mishnath Chassidim*. "The Mishna of the Pious," *i.e.* a Course of Instruction in Holy

[7]

Living. The famous teacher Raba (died 352 C.E.) declared, "Whoever would become pious must fulfil the words of Aboth מילי דאבות." A great non-Jewish scholar and theologian endorses that judgment. "The level of these sayings is very high, and for a knowledge of the ideals of rabbinical ethics and piety, no other easily accessible source is equal to Aboth" (Moore).

Sayings of the Fathers

The appeal of Aboth is widely human and fundamentally Biblical. The Gaon of Wilna and others have shown that every one of the sayings has its roots, or parallel, in Scripture. Aboth is not, however, merely an echo of the gnomic wisdom of the Bible. If, for example, we compare Proverbs 22. 1 ("A good name is rather to be chosen than great riches") with Aboth IV, 17 ("There are three crowns: the crown of learning, the crown of priesthood, and the crown of royalty; but the crown of a good name excels them all"), we find that the latter has a distinct beauty of its own. In the same way, many of the ethical teachings of Scripture are given in Aboth a new and ever memorable setting; *e.g.* "In a place where there are no men, strive thou to be a man." In brief, Aboth is no unworthy continuation of Scripture.

By a sure religious instinct the entire tractate has been early embodied in the Prayer Book. No other *complete* work of any kind—not even the Book of Psalms—has that distinction. The Gaon Rab Amram, in the eighth century, mentions that it was customary in the Babylonian Academies to read one of the chapters of Aboth on Sabbath afternoons. In consequence, the people came to speak of the book as *Pirke Aboth*, "the Chapters of the Fathers"; or, in conversation simply as *Perek*, "the Chapter." Ashkenazi communities today read a chapter, occasionally two, from the Sabbath after

[8]

Passover to the Sabbath before the New Year.

"By this excellent practice, a whole body of moral dicta—each one summing up with remarkable conciseness a life's experience and philosophy, each one breathing the spirit of piety, saintliness, justice, and love for humanity—has sunk deeply into the innermost heart and consciousness of the Jewish people" (Gorfinkle). "Aboth takes rank as a classic in Jewish literature; yet it has never been regarded by Jews as mere literature, as if they had no personal concern with what it said, and were only pleased with the manner of saying it. Aboth speaks to the heart of the Jew in a way and to an extent seldom realized by any non-Jewish reader" (Herford). Sabbath by Sabbath parents studied these wise and edifying maxims with their children, and stressed their moral application; with the result, that the words became part of both Jewish speech and life. The humblest Jewish workman, who had no opportunity for deep Talmudic study, has his Siddur, and was usually well versed in the contents of Aboth reprinted therein. Its influence in moulding the character of the Jew has consequently been as great as it has been beneficent.

Sayings of the Fathers

Aboth has been made the subject of popular and of philosophical commentaries more often than any other of the Rabbinical Writings. Full use has been made of that literature in this latest exposition of wonderful sayings that are universal in application, and have not lost their power with the passing of time. They give guidance in human duty; and the reader of today will find in them light upon many problems of life and conduct.　　　　　THE AUTHOR

A NOTE TO THE AMERICAN READER:

We are honored to bring to the American reader this incomparable commentary on the Pirke Aboth *by the Very Reverend Dr. Joseph H. Hertz, Chief Rabbi of the British Empire.*

Dr. Hertz needs no introduction to an American audience for although he presides over the religious destiny of the United Hebrew Congregation of the British Empire, he is a product of an American Seminary. His commentary on the Pentateuch has achieved the enviable status of a classic in its own day. This commentary on the Pirke Aboth *comes from the second volume of his Prayer Book, a monumental work that will take its place alongside the Pentateuch.*

THE PUBLISHERS.

The text appearing here was reprinted from the Chief Rabbi's edition of the Authorized Daily Prayer Book. Pages referred to but not included in this book will be found in the complete Prayer Book.

Sayings of the Fathers

פִּרְקֵי אָבוֹת :

One of the following chapters is read on each Sabbath from the Sabbath
after פֶּסַח to the Sabbath before רֹאשׁ הַשָּׁנָה.

כָּל־יִשְׂרָאֵל יֵשׁ לָהֶם חֵלֶק לְעוֹלָם הַבָּא · שֶׁנֶּאֱמַר וְעַמֵּךְ כֻּלָם
צַדִּיקִים לְעוֹלָם יִירְשׁוּ אָרֶץ · נֵצֶר מַטָּעַי מַעֲשֵׂה יָדַי לְהִתְפָּאֵר :

פֶּרֶק רִאשׁוֹן :

(א) מֹשֶׁה קִבֵּל תּוֹרָה מִסִּינַי · וּמְסָרָהּ לִיהוֹשֻׁעַ וִיהוֹשֻׁעַ
לִזְקֵנִים וּזְקֵנִים לִנְבִיאִים וּנְבִיאִים מְסָרוּהָ לְאַנְשֵׁי כְנֶסֶת

ALL ISRAEL. This quotation from Mishna Sanhedrin x, 1 is read
before each chapter of Aboth. By studying the teaching contained in
Aboth and following it in his life, every Israelite can become a worthy
member of "the kingdom of priests and a holy nation", and so earn
the reward which is in store for the righteous.

This dogmatic announcement—All Israelites have a portion in the
world to come—closes a long controversy. Many believed that the
number of those who were to share the immortal life was very small.
Sectarian and Jewish-Christian circles held that the vast majority
of mankind were doomed to perdition, unless "saved" by the blood of
a Redeemer. Not so the authoritative Rabbinic opinion as expressed in
this mishna. "The teaching of Hillel concerning the all-sufficing mercy
of God, swept aside the hapless conception that eternal suffering awaits
the average man" (Kohler). And salvation is not conceived by the
Rabbis as confined to Israel. Any heathen who observed the purely
ethical commandments of the Decalogue (see on Genesis 9. 7 in
Genesis, 81, Soncino, 33) was considered "righteous"; and the pro-
nouncement, "The righteous of all peoples have a portion in the World to
come", was early recognized as the universal belief of Judaism.

the world to come. See p. 255.

as it is said. The Sages of Israel did not claim to originate new
religious or ethical doctrines, but to derive them from Scripture ; hence
their custom of adding a proof-text. It must, however, be noted that
the Rabbis, like other preachers, made use of texts for homiletical
purposes, and did not therefore always adhere to the strictly literal
meaning of the Scriptural words.

thy people. The people that by its conduct deserves to have the
Divine Name attached to it.

inherit the land for ever. Employed here in a spiritual sense : the
Abode of the righteous, where death is no more.

I Sayings of the Fathers

1 *One of the following chapters is read on each Sabbath from the Sabbath after Passover until the Sabbath before the New Year.*

All Israel have a portion in the world to come; as it is said, And thy people shall be all righteous; they shall inherit the land for ever, the branch of my planting, the work of my hands, that I may be glorified.

CHAPTER I

1. Moses received the Torah on Sinai, and handed it down to Joshua; Joshua to the elders; the elders to the

---

that I may be glorified. The good life is a hallowing of God, and our acknowledgment of His sovereignty of the universe.

CHAPTER I

1–15. A CHRONOLOGICAL RECORD OF THE ORIGIN AND TRANSMISSION OF THE ORAL TRADITION IN JUDAISM, FROM THE OLDEST RABBINIC AUTHORITIES DOWN TO HILLEL AND SHAMMAI.

1. MOSES. Israel's career as a spiritual force in history begins with the Father of the Prophets, *Mosheh Rabbenu,* "Moses our Teacher", as his People affectionately names him.

Torah. The word "Torah" is variously used for the Pentateuch, the entire Scriptures, the Oral Tradition, as well as for the whole body of religious truth, study and practice. Often the word "Torah" is equivalent to the word "Religion". In this mishna, the reference is to the Oral Tradition. To the Rabbis, the real Torah was not merely the Written Text of the Five Books of Moses (תורה שבכתב); it also included the meaning enshrined in that Text, as expounded and unfolded by the interpretation of successive generations of Sages who made its implicit Divine teachings explicit. This Oral Teaching was handed down from the earliest days by word of mouth (תורה שבעל פה), until it was codified in the Mishna (ca. 200 A.C.E.).

on Sinai. i.e. from God on Sinai.

handed it down. Tradition is a key-word in the Jewish religious system. The Judaism of to-day is in the direct line of descent from the Revelation on Sinai, the intervening generations of teachers forming links in an unbroken chain of Tradition (A. Cohen).

elders. Men of knowledge and experience who, after the death of Joshua, continued to administer Israel and act as its religious guides; Joshua, 24. 31. The term here includes the Judges till Samuel.

הַגְּדוֹלָה · הֵם אָמְרוּ שְׁלשָׁה דְבָרִים · הֱווּ מְתוּנִים בַּדִּין

וְהַעֲמִידוּ תַלְמִידִים הַרְבֵּה וַעֲשׂוּ סְיָג לַתּוֹרָה : (ב) שִׁמְעוֹן

הַצַּדִּיק הָיָה מִשְּׁיָרֵי כְנֶסֶת הַגְּדוֹלָה · הוּא הָיָה אוֹמֵר ·

עַל־שְׁלשָׁה דְבָרִים הָעוֹלָם עוֹמֵד עַל הַתּוֹרָה וְעַל הָעֲבוֹדָה

וְעַל גְּמִילוּת חֲסָדִים : (ג) אַנְטִיגְנוֹס אִישׁ שׂוֹכוֹ קִבֵּל

מִשִּׁמְעוֹן הַצַּדִּיק · הוּא הָיָה אוֹמֵר · אַל־תִּהְיוּ כַּעֲבָדִים

הַמְשַׁמְּשִׁים אֶת־הָרַב עַל־מְנָת לְקַבֵּל פְּרָס · אֶלָּא הֱווּ כַּעֲבָדִים

הַמְשַׁמְּשִׁים אֶת־הָרַב שֶׁלֹּא עַל־מְנָת לְקַבֵּל פְּרָס · וִיהִי מוֹרָא

prophets. The unique band of interpreters of the Divine will, whose writings are an enduring inspiration to the human race.

Great Assembly. Or, " Great Synagogue ". The Prophets, Scribes, Sages and Teachers who continued the spiritual regeneration of Israel that was begun by Ezra. Tradition states that they laid the foundations of the Liturgy, edited several of the books of Scripture, and all but fixed the Biblical canon. Later generations summed up their religious activity in the words : " They restored the crown of the Torah to its pristine splendour ". The main facts concerning the Great Assembly are unassailable by sober historical criticism.

used to say. Were in the habit of saying : these words were their motto.

be deliberate in judgment. Originally an admonition to judges, warning them against hasty decisions. In what is probably a contemporary exposition of Aboth, this maxim was given a wider application : every man is to be moderate in judgment ; *i.e.* refrain from haste, anger, impatience and stubbornness in his dealings with his fellow-men (Aboth di Rabbi Nathan).

raise up many disciples. Judaism is a religious democracy ; and the Torah is the heritage of the *congregation* of Israel ; see p. 13.

a fence round the Torah. Surround it with cautionary rules that shall, like a danger signal, halt a man before he gets within breaking distance of the Divine statute itself. On the Sabbath, for example, even the handling of work-tools is forbidden, מוקצה.

2. *Simon the·Just.* Either Simon ben Onias İ (High Priest from 310 to 291 B.C.E.) ; or, more probably, his grandson (High Priest from 219 to 199). Joshua ben Sira, the contemporary of the latter Simon, speaks of him as, "Great among his brethren and the glory of his people. How glorious was he when he came out of the Sanctuary ! Like the full moon on the feast days, and like the rainbow becoming visible in the cloud " (Ecclesiasticus 50).

[14]

I

2, 3

Sayings
of the
Fathers

prophets ; and the prophets handed it down to the Men of the Great Assembly. They said three things : Be deliberate in judgment ; raise up many disciples ; and make a fence round the Torah.

2. Simon the Just was one of the last survivors of the Great Assembly. He used to say, Upon three things the world is based : upon the Torah, upon Divine service, and upon the practice of charity.

3. Antigonos of Socho received the tradition from Simon the Just. He used to say, Be not like servants who minister to their master upon the condition of receiving a reward ; but be like servants who minister to their master without

upon three things. *i.e.* the neglect of these three things would entail the downfall of all Jewish life. They are Religion, Worship and Humanity.

the Torah. God's Word to Man. It is Israel's "tree of life ". Saadya Gaon, in the tenth century, declared : " Our nation is a nation only by reason of its Torah ".

Divine Service. Originally this meant the sacrificial cult of the Temple, including the prayers by which it was accompanied. But the term soon came to mean " service of God in the heart ", Worship. For the fundamental importance of Prayer—Man's response to God—in Israel, see the Introduction to this Prayer Book.

the practice of charity. Man's recognition of the duties of brotherhood to his fellow-man. The Prophet Micah (6. 8) declared the love of mercy to be one-third of Religion; and the Rabbis held readiness to be helpful to those needing help to be the sign of the Israelite. It is likewise the sign of humanity. " The pitiless man is like the cattle of the field which are indifferent to the sufferings of their kind " (Sefer Chassidim). See p. 16 and 17.

3. *Antigonos.* The first noted Jew with a Greek name. He lived in the first half of the third pre-Christian century.

Socho. Mentioned in Joshua 15. 35.

received. The Hebrew term קבל indicates direct transmission of the Traditional Learning (קבלה).

be not like servants. Serve God from pure motives.

a reward. According to Jewish teaching it is not wrong to hope for God's reward of righteous living ;. see p. 121–128. Even a detractor of Judaism admits that " Piety is not content to stretch out its hands to the empty air—it must meet an Arm descending from heaven. It needs a reward ; not for the reward's sake, but in order to be sure of its own reality ; in order to know that there is a communion of God with

שָׁמַיִם עֲלֵיכֶם: (ד) יוֹסֵי בֶּן־יוֹעֶזֶר אִישׁ צְרֵדָה וְיוֹסֵי בֶּן־
יוֹחָנָן אִישׁ יְרוּשָׁלַיִם קִבְּלוּ מֵהֶם · יוֹסֵי בֶּן־יוֹעֶזֶר אִישׁ
צְרֵדָה אוֹמֵר · יְהִי בֵיתְךָ בֵית וַעַד לַחֲכָמִים וֶהֱוֵה מִתְאַבֵּק
בַּעֲפַר רַגְלֵיהֶם וֶהֱוֵה שׁוֹתֶה בַצָּמָא אֶת־דִּבְרֵיהֶם: (ה) יוֹסֵי
בֶּן־יוֹחָנָן אִישׁ יְרוּשָׁלַיִם אוֹמֵר · יְהִי בֵיתְךָ פָתוּחַ לִרְוָחָה
וְיִהְיוּ עֲנִיִּים בְּנֵי בֵיתֶךָ · וְאַל־תַּרְבֶּה שִׂיחָה עִם הָאִשָּׁה ·
בְּאִשְׁתּוֹ אָמְרוּ קַל וָחֹמֶר בְּאֵשֶׁת חֲבֵרוֹ · מִכַּאן אָמְרוּ חֲכָמִים
כָּל־הַמַּרְבֶּה שִׂיחָה עִם הָאִשָּׁה גּוֹרֵם רָעָה לְעַצְמוֹ וּבוֹטֵל

man, and a road by which to reach it " (Wellhausen). However, Antigonos maintains that, legitimate as the hope of reward may be, it is not
to be the *motive* of our obedience. The Law of God should be kept for
its own sake. " Blessed is the man who fears the Lord, and in His
commandments delights greatly " (Psalm 112. 1); "in His commandments, and not *in the reward* of the commandments ", is the Rabbinic
comment.

the fear of Heaven. The Heb. מורא does not mean *dread* of God. It
denotes the awe and reverence we feel before the Eye that seeth all
things, the Ear that heareth all things, and the Judge before Whom
we are to give account for our doings on earth (III, 1). Renan's render-
ing, " let the dew of Heaven be upon you ", is beautiful but inexact.

4. *José.* An abbreviated form of Joseph. He lived in the first half
of the second pre-Christian century.

Zeredah. Mentioned in Joshua 15. 35.

from the preceding. The Heb. is " from them " ; *i.e.*, either from
Simon and Antigonos, or from the series of unnamed teachers in the
intervening period between Antigonos and José.

From this point to mishna 12, we have the Rabbis named in pairs
(*Zugoth*) : one held the office of *Nasi*, the President of the Sanhedrin (in
English, this is generally spelled with a final *m*—which is quite wrong) ;
and the second was *Av Beth Din*, "father (chief) of the Court of Law."
The appointment of a dual authority seems to have been a revival of
an earlier practice ; II Chronicles 19. 11. The SANHEDRIN was the
Supreme Court and National Council. It consisted of 71 members, and
administered the political, as well as the religious, life of the nation in
the later centuries of the Second Temple. It also dealt with the more
important civil and criminal cases.

the dust of their feet. Disciples as a rule sat on the ground before their
master.

5. *let thy house be open wide.* Wide, as a sign of cordial welcome.
Hospitality to the homeless has always been one of the conspicuous

[16]

I

4, 5

**Sayings
of the
Fathers**

the condition of receiving a reward; and let the fear of
Heaven be upon you.

4. José, the son of Yoezer, of Zeredah, and José, the son
of Yochanan, of Jerusalem, received the tradition from the
preceding. José, the son of Yoezer, of Zeredah, said, Let
thy house be a meeting house for the wise; sit amidst the
dust of their feet; and drink in their words with thirst.

5. José, the son of Yochanan, of Jerusalem, said, Let thy
house be open wide; let the poor be members of thy
household; and engage not in much gossip with women.
This applies even to one's own wife; how much more
then to the wife of one's neighbour. Hence the sages say,
Whoso engages in much gossip with women brings evil upon
himself, neglects the study of the Torah, and will in the
end inherit Gehinnom.

virtues of the Jewish life (Genesis 18). " In the Middle Ages the treat-
ment of poor Jewish travellers was considerate beyond description.
Nothing might be done to put the poor guest to shame " (Abrahams).

members of thy household. The poor are to be treated as if they
were part of the family.

much gossip with women. Nothing derogatory to woman is implied
here. The words " gossip," and especially " much," should be noted.
Some maintain that this maxim belongs to an ethic which modern
thought has outgrown; however, its admonition to avoid not only the
occasion to sin, but everything that might lead to it, will ever retain its
moral value.

this applies. A later marginal note, added by some one who thought
that the maxim needed elucidation.

one's own wife. The reference is here to excessive talk on trivial
matters; for the Rabbis urge a man to discuss his serious concerns with
his wife and profit by her counsel. For the position of woman in
Judaism, see introductory note to the Marriage Service.

how much more. This form of argument is known as *kol v'chomer,*
" from minor to major "; see p. 43.

evil. The danger of immoral conduct. This marginal note finds its
parallel in Ecclesiasticus 9. 9.

Gehinnom. lit. " the valley of Hinnom," situated S.W. of Jerusalem.
In the days of old, it had been the scene of the savage rites connected
with the Canaanite worship of Moloch, to whom children were sacrificed.
The name became a term for what is loathsome and horrifying; and
popular belief in later times identified the locality with the place where
the dead expiate their sins. The name is the opposite of Gan Eden,
" Paradise."

מִדִּבְרֵי תוֹרָה וְסוֹפוֹ יוֹרֵשׁ גֵּיהִנֹּם : (ו) יְהוֹשֻׁעַ בֶּן־פְּרַחְיָה
וְנִתַּי הָאַרְבֵּלִי קִבְּלוּ מֵהֶם · יְהוֹשֻׁעַ בֶּן־פְּרַחְיָה אוֹמֵר · עֲשֵׂה
לְךָ רַב וּקְנֵה לְךָ חָבֵר וֶהֱוֵי דָן אֶת־כָּל־הָאָדָם לְכַף זְכוּת :
(ז) נִתַּי הָאַרְבֵּלִי אוֹמֵר הַרְחֵק מִשָּׁכֵן רָע וְאַל־תִּתְחַבֵּר לְרָשָׁע
וְאַל־תִּתְיָאֵשׁ מִן־הַפֻּרְעָנוּת : (ח) יְהוּדָה בֶּן טַבַּי וְשִׁמְעוֹן
בֶּן־שָׁטַח קִבְּלוּ מֵהֶם · יְהוּדָה בֶּן־טַבַּי אוֹמֵר · אַל־תַּעַשׂ
עַצְמְךָ כְּעוֹרְכֵי הַדַּיָּנִים · וּכְשֶׁיִּהְיוּ בַּעֲלֵי הַדִּין עוֹמְדִים לְפָנֶיךָ

פרקי
אבות

6. *Arbelite.* A native of Arbel, north of Tiberias.

provide thyself a teacher. So as to learn the truths of Religion under competent guidance, and be saved from error and confusion of mind.

get thee a companion. lit. "acquire a companion". Here companionship is recommended for joint religious study. The commentary on Aboth attributed to Rashi, explains this to mean, " acquire books " —the best of companions, and invaluable for the acquisition of religious knowledge. But the saying has an even larger meaning ; namely, win a friend, " one to whom you can reveal all your secrets " (Aboth di Rabbi Nathan). Friendship develops what is best in man ; and everyone can *make* friends, if he tries hard enough. " Either companionship or death," was the prayer of Choni, the Jewish Rip Van Winkle, when he awoke from his sleep of seventy years, and found himself a friendless man in a strange world. The Bible is the Book of Friendship, both in its profound sayings on friendship and the touching examples of it— David and Jonathan, Ruth and Naomi.

charitably. lit. " in the scale of merit." This is one of the great maxims of ethical conduct. " In righteousness shalt thou judge thy neighbour ", is the Divine command (Leviticus 19. 15). Do not judge your suspected fellow-man by appearances, but give him the benefit of the doubt. When weighing what speaks for and against him, incline the balance in his favour. " Whoever judges his fellow in the scale of merit, will be himself similarly judged by God "—say the Rabbis ; and " Great shall be the punishment of a חושד בכשרים, one who suspects, or causes others to suspect, the innocent " ; see p. 2.

7. *keep thee far . . . wicked.* Cf. the morning prayer : " Keep us from a bad man and a bad companion," p. 24. " Woe to the wicked, woe to his neighbour " ; and " the dry wood sets fire to the green ", are two Rabbinic proverbs. A hundred years before Nittai, Ben Sira taught, " He that toucheth pitch shall be defiled " (Ecclesiasticus 13. 1). Nittai's warning may be connected with the clause that follows : when thou seest the wicked profit from their evil ways and escape punishment, be not thou tempted to join them in the hope of the same immunity. The day of reckoning will come.

6. Joshua, the son of Perachyah, and Nittai, the Arbelite, received the tradition from the preceding. Joshua, the son of Perachyah, said, Provide thyself a teacher; get thee a companion; and judge all men charitably.

7. Nittai, the Arbelite, said, Keep thee far from a bad neighbour; associate not with the wicked; and abandon not the belief in retribution.

8. Judah, the son of Tabbai, and Simeon, the son of Shatach, received the tradition from the preceding. Judah, the son of Tabbai, said, (In the judge's office) act not the counsel's part; when the parties to a suit are standing

---

abandon not the belief in retribution. The doctrine of retribution (see p. 121) follows inevitably from the attribute of Divine justice. The conclusion of a modern historian is noteworthy : " One lesson, and only one, history may be said to repeat with distinctness : that the world is built somehow on moral foundations : that in the long run it is well with the good ; in the long run it is ill with the wicked " (Froude).

8. Judah, the son of Tabbai, was among the teachers who fled to Alexandria, because of the persecution of the Pharisees by king Alex ander Jannai (108–76 B.C.E.), a partisan of the Sadducees.

The SADDUCEES were the ruling priestly and aristocratic element during the two centuries preceding the Destruction of Jerusalem in the year 70. They had come under foreign influences, were estranged from the older Jewish life, and chafed under the regulations of the Traditional Law. They denied its authority, as they did the resurrection of the dead, and the continued existence of the soul after death. They were opposed by the PHARISEES—the Scribes and Sages who continued the work of the Men of the Great Assembly. The overwhelming majority of the nation was with the Pharisaic teachers. It is they who built up a purely spiritual worship ; deepened the belief in the immortality of the soul ; and made the Sacred Scriptures the possession of the people. Through their " fences " for the safeguarding of the religious life, they rescued pure monotheism and real morality in their time and for all time. It is unfortunate that these Jewish Puritans have been for 1800 years so maligned by sectarian hatred, that the very name " Pharisee " is often used as a synonym for " hypocrite." Yet they were among the noblest men that ever lived.

act not the counsel's part. Do not suggest to either litigant arguments which he could plead in his behalf : the judge must be impartial. The words may also mean, " Make not thyself like the preparers of the judges " ; *i.e.* men who try to influence the judge before the case is heard, so as to dispose his mind favourably to one party.

are standing before thee. At the hearing of the evidence, the judge must observe equal strictness towards accusers and accused.

יִהְיוּ בְעֵינֶיךָ כִּרְשָׁעִים וּכְשֶׁיִּפָּטְרִים מִלְּפָנֶיךָ יִהְיוּ בְעֵינֶיךָ
כְּזַכָּאִים כְּשֶׁקִּבְּלוּ עֲלֵיהֶם אֶת־הַדִּין : (ט) שִׁמְעוֹן בֶּן־שָׁטַח
אוֹמֵר · הֱוֵי מַרְבֶּה לַחֲקוֹר אֶת־הָעֵדִים · וֶהֱוֵי זָהִיר בִּדְבָרֶיךָ
שֶׁמָּא מִתּוֹכָם יִלְמְדוּ לְשַׁקֵּר : (י) שְׁמַעְיָה וְאַבְטַלְיוֹן קִבְּלוּ
מֵהֶם · שְׁמַעְיָה אוֹמֵר · אֱהַב אֶת־הַמְּלָאכָה וּשְׂנָא אֶת־הָרַבָּנוּת
וְאַל־תִּתְוַדַּע לָרָשׁוּת : (יא) אַבְטַלְיוֹן אוֹמֵר · חֲכָמִים הִזָּהֲרוּ
בְדִבְרֵיכֶם שֶׁמָּא תָחוּבוּ חוֹבַת גָּלוּת וְתִגְלוּ לִמְקוֹם מַיִם

as wicked. Not that he is to assume the accused *guilty* of what he
is charged with doing. In Jewish Law a man is held to be innocent,
until he is *proved* guilty. The judge is merely warned against in any
manner showing favour. "Do not start with the assumption that A is a
man of honour and would not plead falsely ; for, if so, you will not find
him in the wrong, whatever the evidence that comes to light" (Berti-
nora).

Jewish teaching attaches the loftiest ideals to the judicial office.
When acting as judge, a man is the deputy of the Supreme Judge ; and
"he should always imagine that a sword is pointed to his heart, and
Gehinnom yawns at his feet", should he degrade his sacred office. In
a case of a capital offence, circumstantial evidence was rejected. A
sentence of acquittal might be pronounced at once ; but condemnation
might not be pronounced on the day the trial concluded. A Court that
passed a death sentence once in seven years, was known as a Bloody
Assize.

both as innocent. "The sentence of the Court, if just, is adequate to
the case, and clears the score against both litigants" (Herford).

9. *Simeon, the son of Shatach.* His sister Queen Salome Alexandra,
the widow of King Jannai, reigned from 76–67 B.C.E. and he then enjoyed
great influence. He opposed the Sadducees, and made the Pharisaic
party dominant in Israel. Two special achievements ensure him a shining
place in the annals of Israel—the restricting of divorce by new regulations in regard to the *Kesubah* (the Marriage Contract), and the opening
of schools for the young. In his days of poverty, he one day commis-
sioned his disciples to buy him a camel from an Arab. When they
brought him the animal, they gleefully announced that they had found
a precious stone in its collar. "Did the seller know of this" ? he
asked. "Do you think me a barbarian that I should take advantage
of the letter of the law by which the gem is mine together with the
camel ? Return the gem to the Arab immediately". When the heathen
received it back, he exclaimed : "Blessed be the God of Simeon ben

I before thee, let them both be regarded by thee as wicked; but when they are departed from thy presence, regard them both as innocent, the verdict having been acquiesced in by them.

9. Simeon, the son of Shatach, said, Be very searching in the examination of witnesses, and be heedful of thy words, lest through them they learn to falsify.

10. Shemayah and Avtalyon received the tradition from the preceding. Shemayah said, Love work; hate lordship; and seek no intimacy with the ruling power.

11. Avtalyon said, Ye sages, be heedful of your words, lest ye incur the penalty of exile and be exiled to a place

Shatach! Blessed be the God of Israel ". That exclamation of the heathen, we are told, was dearer to him than all the riches of the world. It was a Kiddush Hashem—a Sanctification of the Divine Name.

be very searching. This maxim was probably the fruit of a tragic experience. His son was executed upon a charge which, when too late, was proved to have been groundless ; and closer examination of the witnesses would have revealed the falsity of their evidence.

be heedful of thy words. An injudicious word can suggest to the witness a way of distorting his testimony.

10. *Shemayah and Avtalyon.* According to Tradition they were descendants of proselytes.

love work. Far from looking upon manual labour as a curse, the Rabbis extolled it as an important factor in man's moral education ; and many of the most eminent scholars were manual labourers ; see p. 630. The slowness among Western nations to recognize the dignity of labour is no doubt due to the fact that, till quite recent times, classical literature monopolized the education of the governing classes among European peoples. As with the Greeks and Romans, idleness was for ages the mark of nobility.

hate lordship. Shun office. Hate domineering, playing the superior over your fellows. It hardens the heart, and destroys the finer feelings in him who lords it over others.

the ruling power. He had in mind the local Roman rulers in the days of the later Hasmoneans and of Herod ; but it is never prudent to come under the notice of a despotic government ; see II, 3.

11. *be heedful of your words.* " If sages are to be heedful of their words, how much the more should those who are not sages " (Talmud).

This saying, like the one immediately preceding, is based on the political conditions of Roman Palestine. Avtalyon had witnessed the persecution of the religious teachers under King Alexander Jannai and during the fratricidal conflict of his successors. Many of the teachers had suffered death, others had to flee for their lives into distant lands.

הָרָעִים וְיִשְׁתּוּ הַתַּלְמִידִים הַבָּאִים אַחֲרֵיכֶם וְיָמוּתוּ וְנִמְצָא
שֵׁם שָׁמַיִם מִתְחַלֵּל : (יב) הִלֵּל וְשַׁמַּי קִבְּלוּ מֵהֶם : הִלֵּל
אוֹמֵר הֱוֵה מִתַּלְמִידָיו שֶׁל־אַהֲרֹן אוֹהֵב שָׁלוֹם וְרוֹדֵף שָׁלוֹם
אוֹהֵב אֶת־הַבְּרִיּוֹת וּמְקָרְבָן לַתּוֹרָה : (יג) הוּא הָיָה אוֹמֵר ·
נְגַד שְׁמָא אֲבַד שְׁמָא וּדְלָא מוֹסִיף יָסֵף וּדְלָא יָלֵף קְטָלָא

In such a time—Avtalyon guardedly warns the contemporary teachers
of Judaism—the wise are *circumspect* in their utterances on public
questions. Aside from the peril to their persons, there was real
danger to the Faith. Several of the Sages had fled to Alexandria, the
then capital of the intellectual world, and seething with schools of
fantastic speculation. The disciples of those exiled Sages followed them
to Alexandria ; and there they found a Jewry that had discarded the
Hebrew language, and held the observances and institutions of the
Torah to be mere symbols and allegories. Many of these disciples
succumbed to this Hellenistic Judaism which left its followers nothing
to live by, and nothing to die for. To the pious Palestinian Jew,
Alexandria was indeed " a place of evil waters," a fountain of heresy.

and die. A spiritual death ; they became los to true Judaism.

and the Heavenly Name be profaned. Judaism, as the Revelation
of God, would be discredited by these apostasies—a Chillul Hashem.

12. Hillel and Shammai. The last and most famous of the " pairs ".
They were men of different temperament and methods—Hillel being the
embodiment of humility and kindness, while Shammai lacked patience
and was not of a conciliatory nature. Hillel is the most renowned of the
Rabbis. He rose from the humblest ranks to the highest place in the
Sanhedrin, and founded a dynasty of scholars. His active years were
from 30 B.C.E. to 10 of the Common Era. " He was known as the saint
and the sage who, in his private life and in his dealings with men,
practised the highest virtues of morality and resignation, just as he
taught them in his maxims with unexcelled brevity and earnestness "
(Bacher). The most famous saying of Hillel is, " What is hateful unto
thee, do it not to thy fellow-man ; this is the whole Torah, the rest
is commentary." See " The Golden Rule in Judaism," after Chapter II.

disciples of Aaron. Aaron was the great peace-maker in Rabbinic
legend. He would, in the case of an open rupture between two men, hasten
first to the one, then to the other, saying to each : " If thou didst but
know how he with whom thou hast quarrelled regrets his hard words
to thee " ! With the result, that the former enemies would in their
hearts forgive each other, and as soon as they were again face to face,
would greet each other as friends. His kindness led many a man who
was about to commit a sin, to say to himself, " How shall I be able to lift
up my eyes to Aaron's face ! " Thus did Aaron turn away many from
iniquity ; Malachi 2. 6.

loving peace. An everlasting virtue ; see p. 15–18.

I of evil waters, and the disciples who come after you drink thereof and die, and the Heavenly Name be profaned.

12. Hillel and Shammai received the tradition from the preceding. Hillel said, Be of the disciples of Aaron, loving peace and pursuing peace, loving thy fellow-creatures, and drawing them near to the Torah.

13. He used to say, A name made great is a name destroyed; he who does not increase his knowledge, decreases it; and he who does not study, deserves to die; and he who makes a worldly use of the crown (of the Torah), shall pass away.

thy fellow-creatures. The word *beriyyoth* connotes the whole human family: there is one humanity on earth, even as there is but One God in heaven. The term *beriyyoth* often includes even the brute creation; and to spare animals unnecessary pain is deemed a duty of primary importance צער בעלי חיים מדאורייתא.

drawing them near to the Torah. Hillel did not advocate love of fellow-Jews only, or only of the righteous. He demanded love for all, Jew and non-Jew, those under the Torah and those far from the Torah. Those far from Religion, whether they are within or outside the House of Israel, are to be drawn to it by ways of love and peace. And of such nature was the intensive Jewish propaganda throughout the Roman Empire during the century preceding the fall of Jerusalem. It was primarily the proclamation of the One God, of His Moral Law, and of the Day of Judgment; see p. 144.

13. *he used to say*. This maxim, like the one in II, 7, is in Aramaic, the language of Babylon, where Hillel was born.

a name made great. Fame is usually short-lived, and in his ambition to attain great fame, a man often loses his good name. " Vaulting ambition which o'erleaps itself " (Shakespeare).

increase his knowledge. Study of Torah must be continuous, otherwise what has been learnt will be forgotten.

he who does not study. If a man deliberately refuses to learn aught of Religion, he commits spiritual suicide, and he cannot be regarded as a living member of the House of Israel. Another reading is, " he who does not teach "; *i.e.* he fails to impart the religious knowledge he has. This was deemed an unpardonable sin.

a worldly use of the crown. Of Learning; see IV, 7. A warning against using for worldly advantage any noble gift one possesses. The original word for " crown " is תגא; and various explanations have been given of its exact meaning. Some believe it to be the Latin word *toga*. Hillel's saying would then be, " Anyone who takes to the *toga* (*i.e.* adopts the Roman manner of living, as many of the upper classes did in his day) passes away " from his Faith and People.

חַיָּב וְדִאשְׁתַּמֵּשׁ בְּתָגָא חֲלָף : (יד) הוּא הָיָה אוֹמֵר · אִם
אֵין אֲנִי לִי מִי לִי וּכְשֶׁאֲנִי לְעַצְמִי מָה אֲנִי וְאִם לֹא עַכְשָׁו
אֵימָתָי : (טו) שַׁמַּי אוֹמֵר · עֲשֵׂה תוֹרָתְךָ קֶבַע אֱמוֹר מְעַט
וַעֲשֵׂה הַרְבֵּה וֶהֱוֵה מְקַבֵּל אֶת־כָּל־הָאָדָם בְּסֵבֶר פָּנִים יָפוֹת :
(טז) רַבָּן גַּמְלִיאֵל אוֹמֵר · עֲשֵׂה לְךָ רַב וְהִסְתַּלֵּק מִן הַסָּפֵק
וְאַל־תַּרְבֶּה לְעַשֵּׂר אוּמָדוֹת : (יז) שִׁמְעוֹן בְּנוֹ אוֹמֵר · כָּל־
יָמַי גָּדַלְתִּי בֵּין הַחֲכָמִים וְלֹא מָצָאתִי לַגּוּף טוֹב מִשְּׁתִיקָה
וְלֹא הַמִּדְרָשׁ עִקָּר אֶלָּא הַמַּעֲשֶׂה וְכָל־הַמַּרְבֶּה דְבָרִים מֵבִיא

14. *for myself.* This is far more than merely a rule of worldly wisdom. "If I do not rouse my soul to higher things, who will rouse it?" (Maimonides). Virtue is victory by the individual himself over temptation that assails him. The battle cannot be fought, nor the victory won, by another.

if I am only for myself. Helpfulness is the sign of humanity. It is only a Cain who asks, "Am I my brother's keeper?"

> "Heaven's gate is shut
> To him who comes alone;
> Save thou a soul,
> And *it* shall save thine own!" (Whittier).

if not now, when? Duty's hour is always now, or the opportunity may go forever.

The great moral geniuses of the world have understood to clothe the profoundest truths in simplest language. "Had Hillel left us but this single saying, we should be for ever grateful to him; for scarce anything can be said more briefly, more profoundly, or more earnestly" (H. Ewald).

15. *fix a period.* The study of Torah must not be something casual or occasional.

and do much. "The righteous promise little, and perform much; the wicked promise much, and do not perform even a little" (Talmud).

receive all men with a cheerful countenance. Have a friendly manner in all your dealings with men.

I, 16–II, 8. SAYINGS OF THE MEN OF THE SCHOOL OF HILLEL, AND ADDITIONAL SAYINGS OF HILLEL.

16. *Rabban Gamaliel.* Gamaliel I, who was Hillel's grandson and President of the Great Sanhedrin in the first century. He is the first teacher to bear the superior title *Rabban* ("our Master"). Many 〔24〕

I

14-17

Sayings
of the
Fathers

14. He used to say, If I am not for myself, who will be for me ? And if I am only for myself, what am I ? And if not now, when ?

15. Shammai said, Fix a period for thy study of the Torah ; say little and do much ; and receive all men with a cheerful countenance.

16. Rabban Gamaliel said, Provide thyself a teacher ; be quit of doubt; and accustom not thyself to give tithes by a conjectural estimate.

17. Simeon, his son, said, All my days I have grown up among the wise, and I have found nought of better service than silence ; not learning but doing is the chief thing ; and whoso is profuse of words causes sin.

beneficent regulations are ascribed to him. Among them, the regulation to visit and heal the heathen sick, to bury the friendless dead of heathens, and support their indigent poor in the same way as was done in regard to the Jewish poor, sick and dead. He also laid down the principle, " One must not impose on the public a restriction which the majority cannot endure ". In the Christian Writings, Paul claims to have sat at Gamaliel's feet ; and, in consequence, the latter figures in many Church legends.

provide thyself a teacher. The same phrase as in mishna 6, but here the advice is addressed to one who is himself a teacher or judge. When formulating decisions on questions of law, he should not rely merely upon his own knowledge and judgment, but have another authority whom to consult.

to give tithes by a conjectural estimate. In apportioning the tithe of the produce to be devoted to priests, levites and the poor, the allocation was to be made by exact measure, not by guesswork. " Leave as little scope as possible for personal bias and the temptations of self-interest " (Taylor).

17. *Simeon, his son.* The son of Rabban Gamaliel I. He belonged to the Peace party in the closing years of the Jewish State.

silence. Warnings against loquacity abound in Rabbinic literature. One aphorism reads : "Silence is good for the wise ; how much more so for the foolish " ; cf. " Even a fool, when he holdeth his peace, is counted wise " (Proverbs 17. 28).

not learning but doing. This saying gives expression to a main characteristic of Judaism ; see III, 12, 19 and 22. It does not dispute the high place assigned to learning the Torah : right doing depends on knowing what to do and how to do it. "Study is most important, because it leads to deed ", was the decision of the historic Synod at Lydda, in 133 A.C.E. The aim of the Torah is practical, not theoretical ; above all else its purpose is to regulate conduct. Not

L

חֶטְא : ‏(יח) רַבָּן שִׁמְעוֹן בֶּן־גַּמְלִיאֵל אוֹמֵר ‏· עַל־שְׁלֹשָׁה
דְבָרִים הָעוֹלָם קַיָּם עַל־הָאֱמֶת וְעַל־הַדִּין וְעַל־הַשָּׁלוֹם ‏·
שֶׁנֶּאֱמַר אֱמֶת וּמִשְׁפַּט שָׁלוֹם שִׁפְטוּ בְּשַׁעֲרֵיכֶם :

רַבִּי חֲנַנְיָא בֶּן־עֲקַשְׁיָא אוֹמֵר ‏· רָצָה הַקָּדוֹשׁ בָּרוּךְ הוּא
לְזַכּוֹת אֶת־יִשְׂרָאֵל לְפִיכָךְ הִרְבָּה לָהֶם תּוֹרָה וּמִצְוֹות ‏·
שֶׁנֶּאֱמַר יְיָ חָפֵץ לְמַעַן צִדְקוֹ יַגְדִּיל תּוֹרָה וְיַאְדִּיר :

knowledge, but practice, is of decisive importance; but the practice flows
from knowledge. The Midrash illustrates this by a story, evidently
taken from life, of two muleteers who were enemies. The mule of
one falls beneath its burden; the other sees it, and passes on. But
then he remembers having learned the law of Exodus 23. 5 (" If thou
see the ass of him that hateth thee lying under his burden . . . thou
shalt surely help with him "), and at once he returns and helps the other.
It was the end of their enmity; and it was the knowledge of the Torah
which the one possessed, that yielded this brotherly conduct.

profuse of words causes sin. Based on Proverbs 10. 19, " In
the multitude of words there wanteth not transgression ". A talkative
person is, *e.g.*, liable to become a tale-bearer and slanderer.

18. *Simeon, the son of Gamaliel.* This Gamaliel was the son of
Gamaliel II (who became Patriarch in the year 80) and father of R.
Judah the Prince, the editor of the Mishna. His saying is a variant of
the maxim of Simon the Just (I, 2), and indicates the spiritual forces
by which the social order is held together. Both sayings may be
regarded as new formulations of the Golden Rule.

truth. Truth was called by the Rabbis, " the seal of God ". Truthfulness is of fundamental importance. " Let thy yea be yea, and thy
nay, nay ". The liar is an outcast in Heaven; " he is of those who will
never be admitted to the presence of the Shechinah ". " He who visited
punishment upon the generations of the Flood will call him to account
who breaks his word." The Sages delight in him who is true to his bond,
even when according to the strict letter of the law, he could evade
doing so. " Have thy dealings with thy fellowmen been in truthfulness ? " will be the first question asked on the Judgment Day. Truth
should be spoken *in love :*

> " A truth that's told with bad intent
> Beats all the lies you can invent " (Blake).

I

18

Sayings of the Fathers

18. Rabban Simeon, the son of Gamaliel, said, By three things is the world preserved : by truth, by judgment, and by peace ; as it is said, Judge ye the truth and the judgment of peace in your gates.

Rabbi Chananya, the son of Akashya, said, The Holy One, blessed be he, was pleased to make Israel worthy ; wherefore he gave them a copious Torah and many commandments ; as it is said, It pleased the Lord, for his righteousness' sake, to magnify the Torah and make it honourable.

judgment. For the place of Justice in human life, see *Deuteronomy*, 212–215 (Soncino, 820–822).

Justice is truth in action, in contrast to lawless might. The tragedy of the Jew throughout history is that he has so often been denied justice. Let no Jew, therefore, deny justice to anyone ; and never deprive anyone of life or health, honour or happiness.

peace. For the meaning of this term, see the Priestly Blessing. The symbol of peace is not the cemetery, but the steamship—the harmonizing of conflicting forces towards one goal. A Talmudical comment points out the sequence of ideas : " The three are really one : if judgment is executed, truth is vindicated, and peace results ".

As the reading of each chapter of Aboth is prefaced by the quotation "All Israel " etc., there is also an epilogue to the reading. It is taken from the end of the Mishna tractate *Makkoth.*

Rabbi Chananya. He flourished in the middle of the second century of the Christian Era.

to make Israel worthy. lit. " to make Israel acquire merit ", by giving them opportunity of abundant service and perfect obedience.

copious Torah and many commandments. " These words may be a polemic against the subversive doctrine of Paul concerning the Torah. Here it is asserted that there is no greater proof of God's love to Israel than the multitude of commandments He has given Israel. They were a gracious gift of God, designed to train Israel in moral holiness, and make them all the more worthy in the eyes of the Holy One, blessed be He " (I. Epstein).

his righteousness' sake. Interpreted as " for the sake of Israel's merit."

פֶּרֶק שֵׁנִי :

כָּל יִשְׂרָאֵל וכו'

(א) רַבִּי אוֹמֵר · אֵיזוֹ הִיא דֶרֶךְ יְשָׁרָה שֶׁיָּבוֹר לוֹ הָאָדָם
כָּל־שֶׁהִיא תִפְאֶרֶת לְעֹשָׂהּ וְתִפְאֶרֶת לוֹ מִן הָאָדָם · וֶהֱוֵה
זָהִיר בְּמִצְוָה קַלָּה כְּבַחֲמוּרָה שֶׁאֵין אַתָּה יוֹדֵעַ מַתַּן שְׂכָרָן
שֶׁל־מִצְוֹת · וֶהֱוֵה מְחַשֵּׁב הֶפְסֵד מִצְוָה כְּנֶגֶד שְׂכָרָהּ וּשְׂכַר
עֲבֵרָה כְּנֶגֶד הֶפְסֵדָהּ: הִסְתַּכֵּל בִּשְׁלֹשָׁה דְבָרִים וְאֵין אַתָּה
בָא לִידֵי עֲבֵרָה · דַּע מַה־לְמַעְלָה מִמְּךָ עַיִן רוֹאָה וְאֹזֶן
שׁוֹמַעַת וְכָל־מַעֲשֶׂיךָ בַּסֵּפֶר נִכְתָּבִים : (ב) רַבָּן גַּמְלִיאֵל בְּנוֹ
שֶׁל־רַבִּי יְהוּדָה הַנָּשִׂיא אוֹמֵר · יָפֶה תַלְמוּד תּוֹרָה עִם דֶּרֶךְ

CHAPTER II.

1. *Rabbi.* Judah the Prince (ha-Nasi), the son of Rabban Simeon the Second (I, 18) and a descendant of Hillel in the seventh generation, was born in 135 A.C.E. on the day on which Rabbi Akiba was martyred by the Romans. He died in 219. He was the learned patrician, possessed of great wealth, and enjoying the friendship of members of the Imperial House. In his day, the dignity of the Patriarch of Palestine was little short of that of an actual monarch. In the sphere of his spiritual labours, he made it his aim to ensure unity of religious observance. He collected the decisions and opinions of earlier teachers, noted those which were universally agreed to, and those which were not; and thus at last produced a code of the Traditional Laws that soon attained to canonical rank. This is known as the MISHNA. It is divided into six Orders. The Orders are sub-divided into tractates; tractates into chapters; and chapters into paragraphs—which are each spoken of as a mishna. The first Order deals with Agricultural laws, preceded by *Berachoth*, the tractate on Prayer. The second Order is on Festivals; and the third, on laws of Marriage and Divorce. The fourth is on Civil legislation, and is concluded by *Aboth* as an edifying supplement to this juristic section. The fifth deals with Sanctuary and food laws; and the sixth, with the laws of Clean and unclean. The Mishna became the basis of elucidation—Gemara—both in the Palestinian schools and those of Babylon. The final recensions of these elucidations constitute the Jerusalem Talmud (ca. 350) and the Babylonian Talmud (ca. 500).

II
1, 2
Sayings of the Fathers

"All Israel," etc., p. 13

1. Rabbi said, Which is the right course that a man should choose for himself ? That which is an honour to him who does it, and which also brings him honour from mankind. Be heedful of a light precept as of a grave one, for thou knowest not the grant of reward for each precept. Reckon the loss incurred by the fulfilment of a precept against the reward secured by its observance, and the gain gotten by a transgression against the loss it involves. Reflect upon three things, and thou wilt not come within the power of sin: Know what is above thee—a seeing Eye, and a hearing Ear, and all thy deeds written in a Book.

2. Rabban Gamaliel, the son of Rabbi Judah the Prince, said, An excellent thing is the study of the Torah combined

---

So great was the esteem that his uncommon ability, wide culture and lofty character secured for Rabbi Judah the Prince, that he was known simply as " Rabbi ", or " our holy Master ". The first four paragraphs of this second chapter of Aboth were included in the Code of the Mishna by a later editor.

choose. The conviction that man possesses the power of free-will is basic in Judaism ; cf. III, 19.

that which is an honour to him who does it. That which honours the person who follows it, and wins the approval of his fellow-men. Some Texts read " to his Maker ", instead of " to him who does it "—that which has the approval of God.

honour from mankind. The Rabbis stress the importance of a good reputation ; see III, 13 ; IV, 17.

light precept. A command which does not involve much effort and sacrifice ; or, one for which the penalty of infraction can only be slight. Rabbi is here quoting Ben Azzai ; see IV, 2.

the loss. Through self-denial, or monetary sacrifice. Disregard the cost involved in fulfilling a command, and deem any gain accruing from a transgression as a loss.

a seeing Eye . . . Ear. The safeguard against falling into sin is the thought of God, Who seeth all things, heareth all things, and judgeth the children of men according to their doings.

in a Book. The idea of a Heavenly Book of Records is founded on Exodus 32. 32, Malachi 3. 16, and Daniel 7. 10. For the belief that man himself enters his misdeeds in that Book, see on III, 20

2. *Rabban Gamaliel.* The third who bore that name.

אֶרֶץ שֶׁיְגִיעַת שְׁנֵיהֶם מַשְׁכַּחַת עָוֹן ' וְכָל־תּוֹרָה שֶׁאֵין עִמָּהּ
מְלָאכָה סוֹפָהּ בְּטֵלָה וְגוֹרֶרֶת עָוֹן ' וְכָל־הָעוֹסְקִים עִם־
הַצִּבּוּר יִהְיוּ עוֹסְקִים עִמָּהֶם לְשֵׁם שָׁמַיִם שֶׁזְּכוּת אֲבוֹתָם
מְסַיַּעְתָּם וְצִדְקָתָם עוֹמֶדֶת לָעַד ' וְאַתֶּם מַעֲלֶה אֲנִי עֲלֵיכֶם
שָׂכָר הַרְבֵּה כְּאִלּוּ עֲשִׂיתֶם: (ג) הֱווּ זְהִירִים בִּרְשׁוּת שֶׁאֵין
מְקָרְבִין לוֹ לְאָדָם אֶלָּא לְצֹרֶךְ עַצְמָם ' נִרְאִים כְּאוֹהֲבִים
בִּשְׁעַת הֲנָאָתָם וְאֵין עוֹמְדִים לוֹ לְאָדָם בִּשְׁעַת דָּחֳקוֹ:
(ד) הוּא הָיָה אוֹמֵר ' עֲשֵׂה רְצוֹנוֹ כִּרְצוֹנֶךָ כְּדֵי שֶׁיַּעֲשֶׂה
רְצוֹנְךָ כִּרְצוֹנוֹ ' בַּטֵּל רְצוֹנְךָ מִפְּנֵי רְצוֹנוֹ כְּדֵי שֶׁיְּבַטֵּל רְצוֹן

---

worldly occupation. " The insistence of Jewish Teachers upon the
duty of having a trade or occupation is a mark of that practical sanity
which is pre-eminent in Jewish ethics " (Herford). " The modern
jargon about ' gentlemanly ' occupations gets no countenance from
Judaism. All work is noble that is done nobly " (M. Joseph). No
honest toil, no matter how hard or repugnant, was deemed beneath
the dignity of a scholar, so long as it safeguarded his independence,
and saved him from being a burden on others. Like the Prophets of
old, the Rabbis would take no pay for their teaching or official activi-
ties (see on IV. 7). They were either manual labourers or they followed
some calling or craft. Hillel was a wood-cutter ; Shammai, a builder ;
R. Joshua, a blacksmith ; R. Chanina, a shoemaker ; R. Huna, a
water-carrier ; R. Abba, a tailor ; others were carpenters, tent-makers,
farmers, and merchants ; see I, 10.

makes sin to be forgotten. If the day is filled with honest toil and
the night with study, temptation is robbed of its power. Whereas
complete idleness, the Rabbis rightly hold, leads to wrongdoing and
wrong thinking, sometimes even to mental aberration.

must in the end be futile. Since, in order to maintain himself, he
will have to search for occasional work, which is both uncertain and
unremunerative.

the cause of sin. " He who does not bring up his son to some occupation, is as if he were teaching him robbery " (Talmud).

employed with the congregation. Or, " who occupy themselves with
(the affairs of) the community ".

for Heaven's sake. i.e. " for God's sake " ; an exhortation to disinterested labour. Neither self-aggrandizement nor love of wielding
authority, but the pure desire to promote the welfare of the community, is to guide them in their labours.

with some worldly occupation, for the labour demanded by them both makes sin to be forgotten. All study of the Torah without work, must in the end be futile and become the cause of sin. Let all who are employed with the congregation act with them for Heaven's sake, for then the merit of their fathers sustains them, and their righteousness endures for ever. And as for you, (God will then say,) I account you worthy of great reward, as if you had wrought it all yourselves.

3. Be ye guarded in your relations with the ruling power; for they who exercise it draw no man near to them except for their own interests ; appearing as friends when it is to their own advantage, they stand not by a man in the hour of his need.

4. He used to say, Do His will as if it were thy will, that He may do thy will as if it were His will. Nullify thy will before His will, that He may nullify the will of others before thy will.

merit of their fathers. *Zechuth Ovoth*, see p. 182. The inspiration drawn from the past is an incentive to right action, and increases the zeal, and the achievement, of those engaged upon good work.

their righteousness. When such are the motives behind their efforts, these efforts will lead to enduring results.

as if you had wrought it all yourselves. The faithful workers will not only receive reward for their own labours, but also for the extra good resulting through the influence of ancestral merit.

3. *be ye guarded*. A warning to the communal workers addressed in the preceding mishna, but applicable to all. The character of the Roman officials who administered the Holy Land at that period was such as fully to warrant this bitter comment. However, it is largely true of every " ruling power " ; see on I, 10.

4. *as if it were thy will*. Obey God readily and joyfully, as if you were carrying out your own desires. " Strive to do the will of God, with a perfect heart and a willing soul ; and efface thy will, even if obeying the will of God entail suffering unto thee " (Machzor Vitry).

that He may do thy will. When there is harmony in the relationship between the soul of man and God, man's desires will be worthy of fulfilment on the part of God.

nullify thy will. Should its promptings run counter to His laws and commandments.

the will of others. Who seek to do thee harm.

ב

פרקי
אבות

אֲחֵרִים מִפְּנֵי רְצוֹנֶךָ : (ה) הִלֵּל אוֹמֵר · אַל־תִּפְרוֹשׁ מִן־
הַצִּבּוּר וְאַל־תַּאֲמֵן בְּעַצְמְךָ עַד יוֹם מוֹתְךָ וְאַל־תָּדִין אֶת־
חֲבֵרְךָ עַד שֶׁתַּגִּיעַ לִמְקוֹמוֹ וְאַל־תֹּאמַר דָּבָר שֶׁאִי אֶפְשָׁר
לִשְׁמוֹעַ שֶׁסּוֹפוֹ לְהִשָּׁמֵעַ וְאַל־תֹּאמַר לִכְשֶׁאֶפָּנֶה אֶשְׁנֶה שֶׁמָּא
לֹא תִפָּנֶה : (ו) הוּא הָיָה אוֹמֵר · אֵין בּוֹר יְרֵא חֵטְא וְלֹא
עַם הָאָרֶץ חָסִיד וְלֹא הַבַּיְשָׁן לָמֵד וְלֹא הַקַּפְּדָן מְלַמֵּד וְלֹא
כָּל־הַמַּרְבֶּה בִסְחוֹרָה מַחְכִּים · וּבַמָּקוֹם שֶׁאֵין אֲנָשִׁים הִשְׁתַּדֵּל

THE ORIGINAL CHRONOLOGICAL SEQUENCE, INTERRUPTED BY
I, 16–II, 4, RESUMED.

5. *separate not thyself from the congregation.* Identify your individual
life with that of the community, and stay not apart from it. Share its
weal or woe, and do nothing to undermine its solidarity. Separation
is especially unpardonable when the community is in distress. In the
conflict with Amalek, the hands of Moses grew weary, and they took a
stone and put it under him. " Could they not have given him a chair
or a cushion ? " it is asked. But then Moses said, " Since my brethren
are in trouble, lo, I will bear my part with them ; for he who bears his
portion of the burden, will live to see the hour of consolation " (Talmud).

trust not in thyself. Man must remain on guard against lapse into sin
or heresy throughout his life. The Talmud cites the instance of one who
held the office of High Priest for eighty years, and then became a
Sadducee. Its larger meaning is, " Let no man deem his wisdom perfect,
his knowledge all-embracing, his character unassailable, or his fortune
unchangeable " (Marti).

judge not thy fellow-man. A humane rule of conduct. Do not judge
another till you yourself have come into his circumstances or situation.
" Do not harshly condemn a person who succumbed to temptation until,
faced by a similar temptation, you overcame it " (Rashi). A later
commentator writes, " Do not presume to condemn another, in particular a man who has reached a high office and appears to you not to
be acting correctly. If and when you have reached his position, then
alone will you be in a position to judge " (Rabbi Jonah).

say not anything. Take pains to make your meaning immediately
intelligible to the hearer. A teacher should not utter his doctrine in
an enigmatic form, in the hope that its meaning will eventually become
clear. The original may also be rendered : " Divulge not things that
ought to be kept secret, on the plea that in the end all things are sure
to become public knowledge ".

when I have leisure. A specific application of Hillel's general rule,
" If not now, when ? " (I, 14).

5. Hillel said, Separate not thyself from the congregation ; trust not in thyself until the day of thy death ; judge not thy fellow-man until thou art come into his place ; and say not anything which cannot be understood at once, in the hope that it will be understood in the end ; neither say, When I have leisure I will study ; perchance thou wilt have no leisure.

6. He used to say, An empty-headed man cannot be a sin-fearing man, nor can an ignorant person be truly pious, nor can the diffident learn, nor the passionate teach, nor is everyone who excels in business wise. In a place where there are no men, strive to be a man.

---

6. *empty-headed man.* lit. " a boorish person "—uncultivated and unmannered.

sin-fearing man. " Fear of sin " is the technical term for " the deliberate avoidance of an action that constituted an offence only for the sensitive, but was for the average Jew not deemed a sin " (Büchler); see comment on *pious.*

ignorant person. Heb. *am ha-aretz.* The usual expression for a vulgar person, or for one unlearned in Torah.

pious. Heb. חסיד. Of saintly character ; one who does more than the strict letter of the law requires. Without the beneficent influence of religious knowledge, the ignorant person remains colour-blind to the finer implications of the spiritual life. In Judaism, ignorance is *not* the mother of devotion : only too often is it the mother of desertion.

nor can the diffident. Because he is afraid to ask questions in regard to what is unintelligible to him.

passionate. If the teacher is quick-tempered, he is lacking in patience when interrupted by his pupil's questions. Under such a teacher, obscure points will pass without sufficient explanation.

excels in business. Or, "engrossed in business". Combine a worldly occupation with your Torah-study; but overmuch absorption in business is not as a rule the road to spirituality. Many people look upon a " captain of industry " as the highest embodiment of human wisdom. Hillel assures us, and modern experience confirms his view, that this is quite unjustified.

where there are no men. If a task requires to be done, and there are no other men to do it, it is for us to undertake it. However, in a place where there *is* a man, we must refrain from undue self-assertion. The plain duty then is co-operation or *subordination.* Another explanation is given in Midrash Shemuel : " In a place where no man seeth or knoweth thee, say not, I will sin, as no one seeth or knoweth me. Even when alone, strive to be a man, true and God-fearing ".

לִהְיוֹת אִישׁ : (ז) אַף הוּא רָאָה גֻּלְגֹּלֶת אַחַת שֶׁצָפָה עַל־פְּנֵי
הַמָּיִם ּ אָמַר לָהּ ּ עַל דַּאֲטֵיפְתְּ אַטְיפוּךְ ּ וְסוֹף מְטַיְפַיִךְ
יְטוּפוּן : (ח) הוּא הָיָה אוֹמֵר ּ מַרְבֶּה בָשָׂר מַרְבֶּה רִמָּה ּ
מַרְבֶּה נְכָסִים מַרְבֶּה דְאָגָה ּ מַרְבֶּה נָשִׁים מַרְבֶּה כְשָׁפִים ּ
מַרְבֶּה שְׁפָחוֹת מַרְבֶּה זִמָּה ּ מַרְבֶּה עֲבָדִים מַרְבֶּה גָזֵל ּ
מַרְבֶּה תוֹרָה מַרְבֶּה חַיִּים ּ מַרְבֶּה יְשִׁיבָה מַרְבֶּה חָכְמָה ּ
מַרְבֶּה עֵצָה מַרְבֶּה תְבוּנָה ּ מַרְבֶּה צְדָקָה מַרְבֶּה שָׁלוֹם ּ
קָנָה שֵׁם טוֹב קָנָה לְעַצְמוֹ ּ קָנָה לוֹ דִבְרֵי תוֹרָה קָנָה לוֹ
חַיֵּי הָעוֹלָם הַבָּא : (ט) רַבָּן יוֹחָנָן בֶּן־זַכַּי קִבֵּל מֵהִלֵּל
וּמִשַּׁמַּאי ּ הוּא הָיָה אוֹמֵר ּ אִם לָמַדְתָּ תּוֹרָה הַרְבֵּה אַל־

7. *a skull.* Hillel seems to have known the person whose skull it
was, and he had been a brigand.

because thou drownedst others. They who resort to violence become
victims of violence. Hillel, and the Rabbis after him, clung to the
Biblical belief of retributive justice. " With the measure wherewith
a man measures, shall he be measured." Repentance alone, they held,
could counter-act the operation of this rule. " There are those who
acquire eternal life in years upon years ; there are those who (by repentance) acquire it in an hour ", said Rabbi Judah the Prince.

8. Incisive comments on human nature in the social life of his
time.

flesh . . . worms. A denunciation of gluttony.

property . . . anxiety. Lest he lose it by theft, robbery, or a turn
in his fortunes.

wives . . . witchcraft. Rival wives resorted to witchcraft in order
to retain or regain their husband's affection. Hillel's saying thus con-
demns polygamy. Although polygamy lingered for many centuries after
Hillel, there is no record of a Rabbi having had more than one wife at
one time. About the year 1000, the spiritual leader of European Jewry,
R. Gershom ben Judah, " the Light of the Exile ", declared it pro-
hibited ; and he issued a *cherem* against anyone who, through fraud or
subterfuge, entered upon a polygamous marriage.

maid-servants. Female slaves were not usually of high morality.

men-servants. With rare exceptions, they had no scruples as to
robbing their masters.

the more Torah, the more life. Eternal life. Cf. " for length of days,
and years of life, and peace, shall they add to thee " (Proverbs 3. 2). [34]

7. Moreover, he saw a skull floating on the surface of the water : he said to it, Because thou drownedst others, they have drowned thee ; and, at the last, they that drowned thee shall themselves be drowned.

8. He used to say, The more flesh, the more worms ; the more property, the more anxiety ; the more wives, the more witchcraft ; the more maid-servants, the more lewdness ; the more men-servants, the more robbery ; —the more Torah, the more life ; the more schooling, the more wisdom ; the more counsel, the more understanding ; the more charity, the more peace. He who has acquired a good name, has acquired it for himself ; he who has acquired for himself words of Torah, has acquired for himself life in the world to come.

9. Rabban Yochanan, the son of Zakkai, received the tradition from Hillel and Shammai. He used to say, If

the more schooling. The more opportunities given for corporate study, the greater the ingenuity developed.

the more charity. In later Hebrew, צדקה means " alms-giving ". In reducing the wants of those in need by monetary aid, the harmony of social life is promoted. If we take צדקה in the Biblical sense, and translate it by " righteousness ", the saying echoes the profound declaration of the Prophet, " The work of righteousness shall be peace ; and the effect of righteousness, quietness and confidence for ever " (Isaiah 32. 17).

a good name. The greatest of treasures, but it cannot be transferred to others.

life in the world to come. The effect of Torah-knowledge is the acquisition of merits that outlast this life.

world to come. Heb. *olom ha-bo.* In the Hereafter.

9–21. SAYINGS OF YOCHANAN BEN ZAKKAI AND HIS DISCIPLES.

9. *Yochanan, the son of Zakkai.* When the fall of Jerusalem became certain, he escaped from the city and made his submission to the Romans. He predicted that Vespasian would be elevated to the Imperial throne, and was granted permission to open a school of Rabbinic instruction at Yavneh. This school became the spiritual centre of Jewry ; and by its establishment he rescued Judaism from the shipwreck of the destruction that overwhelmed the Jewish state in the year 70. " Yochanan united within himself the qualities of the prophet Jeremiah and Zerubbabel. Like Jeremiah, he mourned over

ב

תַּחֲזִק טוֹבָה לְעַצְמֶךָ כִּי לְכַךְ נוֹצָרְתָּ : (י) חֲמִשָּׁה תַלְמִידִים
הָיוּ לוֹ לְרַבָּן יוֹחָנָן בֶּן־זַכַּי · וְאֵלּוּ הֵן · רַבִּי אֱלִיעֶזֶר בֶּן־
הוֹרְקְנוֹס רַבִּי יְהוֹשֻׁעַ בֶּן־חֲנַנְיָא רַבִּי יוֹסֵי הַכֹּהֵן רַבִּי
שִׁמְעוֹן בֶּן־נְתַנְאֵל וְרַבִּי אֶלְעָזָר בֶּן־עֲרָךְ : (יא) הוּא הָיָה
מוֹנֶה שִׁבְחָם · אֱלִיעֶזֶר בֶּן־הוֹרְקְנוֹס בּוֹר סוּד שֶׁאֵינוֹ מְאַבֵּד
טִפָּה · יְהוֹשֻׁעַ בֶּן־חֲנַנְיָא אַשְׁרֵי יוֹלַדְתּוֹ · יוֹסֵי הַכֹּהֵן חָסִיד ·
שִׁמְעוֹן בֶּן־נְתַנְאֵל יְרֵא חֵטְא · אֶלְעָזָר בֶּן־עֲרָךְ כְּמַעְיָן הַמִּתְגַּבֵּר :
(יב) הוּא הָיָה אוֹמֵר · אִם יִהְיוּ כָל־חַכְמֵי יִשְׂרָאֵל בְּכַף
מֹאזְנַיִם וֶאֱלִיעֶזֶר בֶּן־הוֹרְקְנוֹס בְּכַף שְׁנִיָּה מַכְרִיעַ אֶת־כֻּלָּם :
אַבָּא שָׁאוּל אוֹמֵר מִשְּׁמוֹ · אִם יִהְיוּ כָל־חַכְמֵי יִשְׂרָאֵל בְּכַף
מֹאזְנַיִם וֶאֱלִיעֶזֶר בֶּן־הוֹרְקְנוֹס אַף עִמָּהֶם וְאֶלְעָזָר בֶּן־עֲרָךְ

the destruction of Jerusalem ; and, like Zerubbabel, he laid the founda-
tion-stone of a new edifice in Judaism " (Graetz).

A disciple of Hillel, Yochanan had a wonderful insight into the
essence of religion. He loved all men, and assigned a supreme place to
charity. To one lamenting the loss of the Temple, he declared : " We
have a means of atonement left that is as effectual as the Temple ;
namely, Lovingkindness. That is now our sin-offering." Again, on his
death-bed, his blessing to his disciples was : " Fear God, as much as
you fear man ". " Not more ? " they asked in surprise. " If you would
but fear Him as much ! " said the dying sage.

ascribe not any merit to thyself. Although to have acquired knowledge
of Torah was praiseworthy, it should not be an occasion for boastful
self-righteousness.

thereunto wast thou created. Thou hast only achieved a purpose in
life that should be the ambition of every Israelite ; merely done thy
duty, and utilized gifts with which God had endowed thee.

10. *five disciples.* Of special excellence; see mishna 15-19.

11. *praise. i.e.* superiority ; the special quality which distinguished
each of his favourite disciples.

cemented cistern. Figurative of a retentive memory. Eliezer won
fame for his exact knowledge of the Traditional teaching handed down
from earlier ages. He was a teacher of Rabbi Akiba.

thou hast learnt much Torah, ascribe not any merit to thyself, for thereunto wast thou created.

10. Rabban Yochanan, the son of Zakkai, had five disciples; and these are they, Rabbi Eliezer, the son of Hyrcanus, Rabbi Joshua, the son of Chananya, Rabbi José, the Priest, Rabbi Simeon, the son of Nathaniel, and Rabbi Elazar, the son of Arach.

11. He used thus to recount their praise : Eliezer, the son of Hyrcanus, is a cemented cistern, which loses not a drop ; Joshua, the son of Chananya—happy is she that bare him ; José, the Priest, is a pious man ; Simeon, the son of Nathaniel, is a fearer of sin ; Elazar, the son of Arach, is like a spring flowing with ever-sustained vigour.

12. He used to say, If all the sages of Israel were in one scale of the balance, and Eliezer, the son of Hyrcanus, in the other, he would outweigh them all. Abba Saul said in his name, If all the sages of Israel, together with Eliezer, the son of Hyrcanus, were in one scale of the balance, and Elazar, the son of Arach, in the other scale, he would outweigh them all.

happy is she that bare him. What a life of benignity and blessing must it have been, to have elicited such praise from a statesman, scholar and saint like Rabban Yochanan !

pious man. *i.e.*, one who shows particular heedfulness in matters of mine and thine ; see mishna 17.

fearer of sin. See mishna 6.

a spring. In contrast to a " cemented cistern ", he had an original mind which overflowed with new ideas.

12. *if all the sages.* Yochanan set the higher value on the accurate preservation • of the Traditional lore, as against acute argumentative power ; and, for that reason, praised the pre-eminence of Eliezer.

Abba Saul. He was a contemporary of R. Judah the Prince. "Abba ", Aramaic for " father ", was a title of affection given to several Rabbis. He cited another tradition of Yochanan's estimate, and thus awarded the palm to Elazar ben Arach : the critical and original mind, rather than the retentive memory, was given preference.

בְּכַף שְׁנֵיהֶ מַכְרִיעַ אֶת־כֻּלָּם : (יג) אָמַר לָהֶם · צְאוּ וּרְאוּ
אֵיזוֹ הִיא דֶּרֶךְ טוֹבָה שֶׁיִּדְבַּק בָּהּ הָאָדָם · רַבִּי אֱלִיעֶזֶר
אוֹמֵר עַיִן טוֹבָה רַבִּי יְהוֹשֻׁעַ אוֹמֵר חָבֵר טוֹב רַבִּי יוֹסֵי
אוֹמֵר שָׁכֵן טוֹב רַבִּי שִׁמְעוֹן אוֹמֵר הָרוֹאֶה אֶת־הַנּוֹלָד רַבִּי
אֶלְעָזָר אוֹמֵר לֵב טוֹב: אָמַר לָהֶם · רוֹאֶה אֲנִי אֶת־דִּבְרֵי
אֶלְעָזָר בֶּן־עֲרָךְ מִדִּבְרֵיכֶם שֶׁבִּכְלָל דְּבָרָיו דִּבְרֵיכֶם :
(יד) אָמַר לָהֶם · צְאוּ וּרְאוּ אֵיזוֹ הִיא דֶּרֶךְ רָעָה שֶׁיִּתְרַחֵק
מִמֶּנָּה הָאָדָם · רַבִּי אֱלִיעֶזֶר אוֹמֵר עַיִן רָעָה רַבִּי יְהוֹשֻׁעַ
אוֹמֵר חָבֵר רָע רַבִּי יוֹסֵי אוֹמֵר שָׁכֵן רָע רַבִּי שִׁמְעוֹן אוֹמֵר
הַלֹּוֶה וְאֵינוֹ מְשַׁלֵּם · אֶחָד הַלֹּוֶה מִן־הָאָדָם כְּלֹוֶה מִן־הַמָּקוֹם ·
שֶׁנֶּאֱמַר לֹוֶה רָשָׁע וְלֹא יְשַׁלֵּם וְצַדִּיק חוֹנֵן וְנוֹתֵן · רַבִּי
אֶלְעָזָר אוֹמֵר לֵב רָע : אָמַר לָהֶם · רוֹאֶה אֲנִי אֶת־דִּבְרֵי
אֶלְעָזָר בֶּן־עֲרָךְ מִדִּבְרֵיכֶם שֶׁבִּכְלָל דְּבָרָיו דִּבְרֵיכֶם :
(טו) הֵם אָמְרוּ שְׁלֹשָׁה דְבָרִים · רַבִּי אֱלִיעֶזֶר אוֹמֵר · יְהִי
כְבוֹד חֲבֵרְךָ חָבִיב עָלֶיךָ כְּשֶׁלָּךְ וְאַל־תְּהִי נוֹחַ לִכְעוֹס

---

13. *he said.* *i.e.* Rabban Yochanan.

go forth and see. Or, " behold now " ; a phrase for arousing attention
to a question.

the good way. What good quality shall a man cleave to as the essential
of a good life ? What is the clue to right living ?

a good eye. The kindly eye, blessed with the quality of seeing the
good in other people, and free from envy and ill-will; cf. v, 22.

a good friend. This means primarily, to *be* a good friend.

a good neighbour. *i.e.* the possession of the attributes which make
one a good neighbour, a worthy member of society.

one who foresees. The effect of his actions before performing them.

a good heart. *i.e.* unselfish love in thought, feeling and deed. In
Hebrew the heart is the source of feeling and action, as well as the seat of
understanding. " The heart sees, hears, speaks ; the heart rejoices,
weeps, breaks and rebels ; the heart invents, suspects, desires, loves and

13. He said to them, Go forth and see which is the good way to which a man should cleave. R. Eliezer said, A good eye; R. Joshua said, A good friend; R. José said, A good neighbour; R. Simeon said, One who foresees the fruit of an action; R. Elazar said, A good heart. Thereupon he said to them, I approve the words of Elazar, the son of Arach, rather than your words, for in his words yours are included.

14. He said to them, Go forth and see which is the evil way that a man should shun. R. Eliezer said, An evil eye; R. Joshua said, A bad friend; R. José said, A bad neighbour; R. Simeon said, One who borrows and does not repay. (He that borrows from man is the same as if he borrowed from God; as it is said, The wicked borroweth, and payeth not again, but the righteous dealeth graciously and giveth); R. Elazar said, A bad heart. Thereupon he said to them, I approve the words of Elazar, the son of Arach, rather than your words, for in his words yours are included.

15. They each said three things. R. Eliezer said, Let the honour of thy fellow-man be as dear to thee as thine own; be not easily moved to anger; and repent one

hates; meditates, schemes and obeys " (Midrash). If the heart is good, it will prompt only right action.

14. *an evil eye.* Stands for envy, ill-will, niggardliness.

one who borrows and does not repay. Such a one does *not* foresee the future, and is blind to the consequences of his conduct.

borrows from man. This clause is probably an editorial comment. One who lacks foresight and incurs responsibilities which he is unable to meet, borrows from God; seeing that wealth comes from Him, and men are merely His stewards.

and giveth. *i.e.* he repays the lender for his act of kindness.

15. *let the honour.* Far beyond other moralists, the Rabbis sternly condemn any action or word that injures a man's reputation or exposes him to contempt or derision. The sin increases in gravity when one benefits by such disgrace of his fellowman. "He who elevates himself at the expense of his neighbour's degradation, has no share in the World to come " (Talmud).

וְשׁוּב יוֹם אֶחָד לִפְנֵי מִיתָתְךָ וֶהֱוֵה מִתְחַמֵּם כְּנֶגֶד אוּרָן
שֶׁל־חֲכָמִים וֶהֱוֵי זָהִיר בְּנַחַלְתָּן שֶׁלֹּא תִכָּוֶה ' שֶׁנְּשִׁיכָתָן
נְשִׁיכַת שׁוּעָל וַעֲקִיצָתָן עֲקִיצַת עַקְרָב וּלְחִישָׁתָן לְחִישַׁת
שָׂרָף וְכָל־דִּבְרֵיהֶם כְּגַחֲלֵי אֵשׁ : (טז) רַבִּי יְהוֹשֻׁעַ אוֹמֵר '
עַיִן הָרָע וְיֵצֶר הָרָע וְשִׂנְאַת הַבְּרִיּוֹת מוֹצִיאִים אֶת־הָאָדָם
מִן־הָעוֹלָם : (יז) רַבִּי יוֹסֵי אוֹמֵר ' יְהִי מָמוֹן חֲבֵרְךָ חָבִיב
עָלֶיךָ כְּשֶׁלָּךְ וְהַתְקֵן עַצְמְךָ לִלְמוֹד תּוֹרָה שֶׁאֵינָהּ יְרֻשָּׁה
לָךְ וְכָל־מַעֲשֶׂיךָ יִהְיוּ לְשֵׁם שָׁמָיִם : (יח) רַבִּי שִׁמְעוֹן אוֹמֵר '

be not easily moved to anger. " Whosoever gives way to anger, if he
is wise, his wisdom leaves him ; if he is a prophet, the spirit of Prophecy
forsakes him. He who breaks anything in his anger, is as if he were
an idolater " (Talmud). Anger is a blind emotional reaction to an
injury received. Thus, when a child hurts its foot against a stone,
it is often so unreasonably angry as to strike the stone. Altogether
different is the moral feeling of *indignation* that sweeps over us whenever we see a great wrong committed; not because it injures *us*, as is
always the case in anger, but because the wrong is an outrage against
justice and right. See also R. Eliezer's prayer, p. xxi.

repent one day before thy death. When R. Eliezer gave this exhortation to his disciples, they asked, " But does a man know the day of
his death ? " He replied, " Let him then repent to-day, lest he die
to-morrow "; see p. 138.

the fire of the wise. One who wishes to warm himself, remains a certain
distance from the fire ; if he approaches too near, he is burned. So,
do not endeavour to become too intimate with the Wise. R. Eliezer was
excommunicated by his colleagues because he refused to accept the ruling
of the majority, and he died under the ban. There is much suppressed
passion in his words, " which do not deny to his opponents a measure
of justification" (Graetz). "As a piece of self-revelation, they awaken
sympathy for a great man suffering in lonely bitterness " (Herford).

16. Rabbi Joshua ben Chananya was the " man of the golden
mean " in the School of Yavneh. Of great gentleness and ready wit,
he was averse to extravagant measures, whether in religion or in life.
He is the author of the universalist doctrine, " The righteous of all
nations have a share in the World to come ". He visited Rome in 95,
and by his balanced and calm character exercised a restraining influence
in all dealings with the authorities. In addition to his Rabbinical
erudition, he was possessed of considerable astronomical knowledge. **[40]**

II

16, 17

Sayings
of the
Fathers

day before thy death. And (he further said), Warm thyself ⁻
by the fire of the wise ; but beware of their glowing coals,
lest thou be burnt, for their bite is the bite of the fox,
and their sting is the scorpion's sting, and their hiss is the
serpent's hiss, and all their words are like coals of fire.

16. R. Joshua said, The ·evil eye, the evil inclination,
and hatred of his fellow-creatures drive a man out of the
world.

17. R. José said, Let the property of thy fellow-man
be as dear to thee as thine own ; qualify thyself for
the study of the Torah, since the knowledge of it is not an
inheritance of thine ; and let all thy deeds be done for the
sake of Heaven.

Thus he seems to have known, and foreseen the reappearance, of what
many believe to have been Halley's comet.

the evil eye. An envious disposition ; see on mishna 14.

the evil inclination. See p. 25. Man's natural instincts, when un-
controlled, lead to sin, and ruin a man's life.

hatred of his fellow-creatures. Misanthropy, contempt for your
fellow-men. For " fellow-creatures " (*beriyyoth*), see on I, 12.

drive a man out of the world. Means either shorten his life ; or,
preferably, cut him off from human society.

17. *fellow-man.* Another application of the Golden Rule : respect
your fellow-man's property rights as you would desire yours to be
respected ; see mishna 15 and v, 13.

qualify thyself. Or, " prepare thyself ". As in the case of prayer,
the study of the Torah must be approached with a mind properly
attuned to a sacred purpose.

not an inheritance of thine. i.e. the actual knowledge may only be
acquired by personal effort ; it cannot be bequeathed or inherited.

all thy deeds be done for the sake of Heaven. Even the common actions
of daily life should be consecrated to the service of God, and be hallowed
by Religion. Thus, Hillel told his disciples that to keep the body physically clean by bathing, was a religious duty.

> " Teach me, my God and King,
> In all things Thee to see ;
> And what I do in any thing,
> To do it as for Thee.
>
> A servant with this clause
> Makes drudgery divine ;
> Who sweeps a room as for Thy laws,
> Makes that and the action fine " (Herbert).

הֱוֵה זָהִיר בִּקְרִיאַת שְׁמַע וּבִתְפִלָּה וּכְשֶׁאַתָּה מִתְפַּלֵּל אַל־
תַּעַשׂ תְּפִלָּתְךָ קֶבַע אֶלָּא רַחֲמִים וְתַחֲנוּנִים לִפְנֵי הַמָּקוֹם ·
שֶׁנֶּאֱמַר כִּי־חַנּוּן וְרַחוּם הוּא אֶרֶךְ אַפַּיִם וְרַב־חֶסֶד וְנִחָם
עַל־הָרָעָה · וְאַל־תְּהִי רָשָׁע בִּפְנֵי עַצְמֶךָ : (יט) רַבִּי אֶלְעָזָר
אוֹמֵר · הֱוֵה שָׁקוּד לִלְמוֹד תּוֹרָה וְדַע מַה־שֶּׁתָּשִׁיב
לָאֶפִּיקוֹרוֹס וְדַע לִפְנֵי מִי אַתָּה עָמֵל וּמִי הוּא בַּעַל מְלַאכְתְּךָ
שֶׁיְּשַׁלֶּם־לְךָ שְׂכַר פְּעֻלָּתֶךָ : (כ) רַבִּי טַרְפוֹן אוֹמֵר · הַיּוֹם
קָצֵר וְהַמְּלָאכָה מְרֻבָּה וְהַפּוֹעֲלִים עֲצֵלִים וְהַשָּׂכָר הַרְבֵּה

ב
פרקי
אבות

18. *be careful to read the Shema.* see p. 116 f.
and to say the Amidah. See p. 130.
as a fixed mechanical task. Prescribed prayers are not to be offered
in a perfunctory way. The Rabbis who created the Liturgy taught the
loftiest conception of prayer. See p. xxi and xxii.
be not wicked in thine own esteem. This saying preaches the duty of
self-respect. Do not think yourself so abandoned that it is useless for
you to make " an appeal for mercy and grace " before God. " Regard
not thyself as wholly wicked, since by so doing thou givest up hope of
repentance " (Maimonides). Communities, like individuals, are under the
obligation not to be wicked in their own esteem. Achad Ha-am wrote :
" Nothing is more dangerous for a nation or for an individual than
to plead guilty to imaginary sins. Where the sin is real—by honest
endeavour the sinner can purify himself. But when a man has been per-
suaded to suspect himself unjustly—what *can* he do ? Our greatest
need is emancipation from self-contempt, from this idea that we are
really worse than all the world. Otherwise, we may in course of time
become in reality what we now imagine ourselves to be."
19. *be eager.* Without enthusiasm, the constant application essential
for study will wane.
know what answer. It is a duty to fit oneself for the duty of defend-
ing the honour of Judaism against ignorant or malicious opponents.
unbeliever. Heb. *apikouros*, the Hebraized Greek form for a
follower of Epicurus. That philosopher denied that God took any notice
of human beings, or that He cared in the least whether their conduct
was righteous or otherwise. Such denial of a Heavenly Judge and a
Judgment Day is in Judaism the cardinal sin. Hence his name was
chosen as a synonym for sceptic or heretic.
know. Be conscious that you are working " for the Name of
Heaven ". The quality of your effort will be influenced by that consciousness.

18. R. Simeon said, Be careful to read the Shema, and to say the Amidah; and when thou prayest, regard not thy prayer as a fixed mechanical task, but as an appeal for mercy and grace before the All-present (as it is said, For he is gracious and full of mercy, slow to anger, and abounding in lovingkindness, and relenteth him of the evil); and be not wicked in thine own esteem.

19. R. Elazar said, Be eager to learn Torah; know what answer to give to the unbeliever; know also before whom thou toilest, and who thy Employer is, who will pay thee the reward of thy labour.

20. Rabbi Tarfon said, The day is short, and the work is great, and the labourers are sluggish, and the reward is much, and the Master is urgent.

---

20. *Rabbi Tarfon.* Of priestly descent, he had officiated in the Temple. Though not a disciple of Rabban Yochanan, he was his contemporary. Of stern and rigid temperament, his was a nature of true religious delicacy and refinement. One Sabbath day, his mother's sandals split; and as she could not mend them and would have to walk across the courtyard barefoot, Tarfon kept stretching his hands under her feet, so that she might walk over them all the way: he out-did Sir Walter Raleigh in chivalry. His best-known saying, here given, is of great solemnity and beauty.

the day is short. The life of man, or that part of it between childhood (dawn) and old age (evening) when it is possible to work with full vigour, is but of brief duration. But man is neither to despair nor yield to idleness.

the work. The utilization of life's opportunities in the service of God.

is great. Therefore time is too precious to waste.

labourers. God's creatures.

sluggish. There is in man a tendency to negligence and indolence that requires conscious effort to overcome; see III, 14.

reward. Although the ideal is to work from a sense of duty, reward awaits the loyal toiler; see on I, 3.

the Master. lit. " the master of the house ", the universal Father Who has the right to demand the labour of the members of His household, mankind.

urgent. It will brook no delay: " If not now, when ? "

It has been suggested that the first clause of the Hebrew might originally have been היום קציר *to-day is harvest time*: the work is great, the labourers are sluggish, the reward is much, and the Master is urgent!

ב

וּבָעַל הַבַּיִת דּוֹחֵק : (כא) הוּא הָיָה אוֹמֵר · לֹא עָלֶיךָ
הַמְּלָאכָה לִגְמוֹר וְלֹא־אַתָּה בֶּן־חוֹרִין לְהִבָּטֵל מִמֶּנָּה · אִם
לָמַדְתָּ תּוֹרָה הַרְבֵּה נוֹתְנִים לְךָ שָׂכָר הַרְבֵּה וְנֶאֱמָן הוּא
בַּעַל מְלַאכְתְּךָ שֶׁיְשַׁלֶּם לְךָ שְׂכַר פְּעֻלָּתֶךָ · וְדַע שֶׁמַּתַּן
שְׂכָרָם שֶׁל־צַדִּיקִים לֶעָתִיד לָבוֹא :

רַבִּי חֲנַנְיָא בֶּן־עֲקַשְׁיָא וכו׳

21. *to complete the work.* It may not be given thee to complete the
task called for, but that is no reason why it should not be attempted.
Be not disheartened by the greatness and difficulty of what is before
thee. Do as much as is in thy power.

THE " GOLDEN RULE " IN JUDAISM.

The world at large is unaware of the fact that the sublime
maxim of morality, "Thou shalt love thy neighbour as thyself" (Leviticus 19. 18)—was first taught by Judaism. No less a thinker than John
Stuart Mill expressed his surprise that it came from the Pentateuch.
Not only is it Jewish in origin, but, long before the rise of Christianity,
Israel's religious teachers quoted it, either verbally or in paraphrase, as
expressing the essence of the moral life. Thus, Ben Sira says, " Honour
thy neighbour as thyself"; and, a hundred years later, the Testaments
of the Twelve Patriarchs declares, " A man should not do to his neighbour what a man does not desire for himself ". Tobit admonishes his
son in the words, " What is displeasing to thyself, that do not unto any
other ". Philo and Josephus have sayings similar to the above. As to
the Rabbis, there is the well-known story of Hillel and the heathen
scoffer who asked him to condense for him the whole Torah in briefest
possible form. Hillel's answer is, " Whatever is hateful unto thee, do
it not unto thy fellow : this is the whole Torah ; the rest is explanation".
In the generation after the Destruction of the Temple, Rabbi Akiba
declares, "*Thou shalt love thy neighbour as thyself* is a fundamental
rule in the Torah ". " All men are created in the Divine image," says
his contemporary Ben Azzai ; " and, therefore, all are our fellowmen,
and entitled to human love ".

And the command of Leviticus 19. 18 applies to classes and nations
as well as to individuals. The Prophets in their day, on the one hand,
arraigned the rich for their oppression of the poor ; and, on the other
hand, pilloried the nations that were guilty of inhumanity and breach
of faith towards one another. Of Rabbinic opinion in all times, the
following saying of Judah the Pious (see p. 214) is typical : " On the
Judgment Day, the Holy One, blessed be He, will call the nations
to account for every violation of the command ' Thou shalt love

[44]

21. He used also to say, It is not thy duty to complete the work, but neither art thou free to desist from it ; if thou hast studied much Torah, much reward will be given thee, for faithful is thy Employer to pay thee the reward of thy labour ; and know that the grant of reward unto the righteous will be in the time to come.

" Rabbi Chananya ", etc., p. 27

thy neighbour as thyself' of which they have been guilty in their dealings with one another ".

Though the Founder of Christianity quotes " Thou shalt love thy neighbour as thyself " as the old Biblical command of recognized central importance, nevertheless Christian theologians maintain that its morality is only tribal, alleging that the Hebrew word for "neighbour" (*rea*) refers only to the fellow-Israelite. This is incorrect. One need not be a Hebrew scholar to convince oneself of the fact that *rea* means neighbour of whatever race or creed. Thus, in Exodus 11. 12, " Let them ask every man of his neighbour and every woman of her neighbour "—the Hebrew word for *neighbour* cannot possibly mean " fellow-Israelite ", but distinctly refers to the Egyptians. In order to prevent any possible misunderstanding, the command of love of neighbour is, in *v.* 34 of that same nineteenth chapter of Leviticus, extended to include the homeless alien :—

" The stranger that sojourneth with you shall be unto you as the homeborn among you, and thou shalt love him as thyself."

The word " neighbour " in Leviticus 19. 18 is thus equivalent to "fellow-man ", and it includes in its range every human being by virtue of his humanity. " The commandment to love one's fellow-man ", said Rabba, a Babylonian teacher in the third century, " must be observed even in the execution of a criminal, and he should be granted as easy a death as possible ". In Jerusalem, the criminal before being led to execution was given a drugged cup of wine, by which he lost consciousness of what was being done to him. Quite other was the spirit of Rome. The Romans invented the fiendish punishment of crucifixion, which prolonged the death agonies of the victims for days. If Jewish teaching and Jewish example had been heeded, the history of torture in European history would have been far less voluminous than it is.

Christian theologians stress the fact that both the Book of Tobit and Hillel paraphrase Leviticus 19. 18 in a negative way—" Whatever is hateful unto thee, do it not unto thy fellow " : and they, therefore, maintain that the Jewish Golden Rule is merely a " negative " Golden Rule. This argument is illusory. In the oldest Christian literature, the two forms are recorded indiscriminately. The negative Golden Rule occurs in the Western texts of Acts 15. 20, Romans 13. 10, the Teaching of the Twelve Apostles, and the Apostolical Constitutions; and positive forms of the Rule have had a place in Judaism. Thus Hillel says, "Love thy fellow-creatures " : and Eliezer ben Hyrcanus,

פֶּרֶק שְׁלִישִׁי :

כָּל יִשְׂרָאֵל וכו׳

(א) עֲקַבְיָא בֶּן־מַהֲלַלְאֵל אוֹמֵר הִסְתַּכֵּל בִּשְׁלשָׁה דְבָרִים
וְאֵין אַתָּה בָא לִידֵי עֲבֵרָה דַּע מֵאַיִן בָּאתָ וּלְאָן אַתָּה הוֹלֵךְ
וְלִפְנֵי מִי אַתָּה עָתִיד לִתֵּן דִּין וְחֶשְׁבּוֹן ' מֵאַיִן בָּאתָ מִטִּפָּה
סְרוּחָה ' וּלְאָן אַתָּה הוֹלֵךְ לִמְקוֹם עָפָר רִמָּה וְתוֹלֵעָה '
וְלִפְנֵי מִי אַתָּה עָתִיד לִתֵּן דִּין וְחֶשְׁבּוֹן לִפְנֵי מֶלֶךְ מַלְכֵי
הַמְּלָכִים הַקָּדוֹשׁ בָּרוּךְ הוּא : (ב) רַבִּי חֲנִינָא סְגַן הַכֹּהֲנִים
אוֹמֵר ' הֱוֵי מִתְפַּלֵּל בִּשְׁלוֹמָהּ שֶׁל־מַלְכוּת שֶׁאִלְמָלֵא מוֹרָאָהּ
אִישׁ אֶת־רֵעֵהוּ חַיִּים בְּלָעוֹ : (ג) רַבִּי חֲנַנְיָא בֶּן־תְּרַדְיוֹן

" Let the honour of thy fellow-man be as dear to thee as thine own ".
But the mere fact that Leviticus 19. 18 is itself positive, renders all
talk of a "negative" Jewish morality in connection with the Golden Rule
fatuous.

One word more. Noble as is the Golden Rule, it is only *part* of the
ethical and social legislation of the Torah. "Condensations of the
essentials of the moral law into one comprehensive rule, are of interest as
exhibiting a sound estimate of religious and moral values. For the actual
conduct of life, and above all for the practical morals of a community or
a people in any age, explicit rules, defining cases and prescribing what
is to be done in concrete instances, are indispensable" (Moore).

CHAPTER III.
SAYINGS OF AKIBA AND OTHERS.

The sayings in this chapter are not in chronological order.

1. *Akavya.* A contemporary of Hillel. He was offered the position
of Av Beth Din (see on I, 4) after Shammai's death, on condition that he
retracted certain opinions he had expressed ; but he refused to do so.
" Let not men say that, for the sake of office, I changed my views."
When, on his death-bed, his son asked that he recommend him to his
friends, he answered : " It is thy deeds that will bring thee near to men,
and thy deeds that will drive thee from them ".

reflect. Sinfulness is the result of pride, and of thoughtlessness as
to what follows death. If a man remembers whence he comes, he is
rendered humble. If he considers whither he is going, he is saved from
passion and the lust for money. And if he bears in mind the Tribunal

[46]

CHAPTER III

"All Israel ", etc., p. 13

1. Akavya, the son of Mahalalel, said, Reflect upon three things, and thou wilt not come within the power of sin : know whence thou camest, whither thou art going ; and before whom thou wilt in future have to give account and reckoning. Whence thou camest :—from a fetid drop ; whither thou art going :—to a place of dust, worms and maggots ; and before whom thou wilt in future have to give account and reckoning :—before the Supreme King of kings, the Holy One, blessed be he.

2. R. Chanina, the Vice-High-Priest, said, Pray for the welfare of the government, since but for the fear thereof men would swallow each other alive.

3. R. Chananya, the son of Teradyon, said, If two sit together and interchange no words of Torah, they are a meeting of scoffers, concerning whom it is said, The godly man sitteth not in the seat of the scoffers ; but if two sit

before Whom he is to appear, he will flee sin. See II, 1.

place of dust. Cf. "dust thou art, and unto dust shalt thou return " (Genesis 3. 19).

2. *Vice-High Priest.* A deputy for the High Priest, to take his place should the latter be prevented from discharging his functions.

pray for the welfare of the government. See p. 503. The " government " was Rome ; and, although it was harsh in its administration, he advised his fellow-Jews not to work for a breach with Rome. His seems to have been the attitude of the conservative priesthood in the political controversy which preceded the Great War against Rome in 66-70.

swallow each other alive. Government stands for order ; and without it there would be the chaos of anarchy ; cf. Shakespeare, " You cry against the noble Senate, who . . . . keep you in awe, which else would feed on one another " (Coriolanus I, 1, 188–192).

MISHNA 3, 4 and 7. Conversation must be hallowed in thought and speech by remembrance of the Divine Presence. The texts quoted are applied in the homiletic manner of the Haggadists of that generation.

3. *Chananya.* He was the father of Beruria, the renowned wife of Rabbi Meir ; see p. 588. He suffered martyrdom in the Second War against Rome, after the defeat of Bar Cochba in the year 135, of the Christian era. The Romans were masters in torture. He was wrapped in a Scroll of the Torah, and then set fire to ; and to prolong his sufferings, moist wool was placed over his heart. His dying words were

אוֹמֵר · שְׁנַיִם שֶׁיּוֹשְׁבִים וְאֵין בֵּינֵיהֶם דִּבְרֵי תוֹרָה הֲרֵי זֶה
מוֹשַׁב לֵצִים · שֶׁנֶּאֱמַר וּבְמוֹשַׁב לֵצִים לֹא יָשָׁב · אֲבָל שְׁנַיִם
שֶׁיּוֹשְׁבִים וְיֵשׁ בֵּינֵיהֶם דִּבְרֵי תוֹרָה שְׁכִינָה שְׁרוּיָה בֵינֵיהֶם ·
שֶׁנֶּאֱמַר אָז נִדְבְּרוּ יִרְאֵי יְיָ אִישׁ אֶל־רֵעֵהוּ וַיַּקְשֵׁב יְיָ וַיִּשְׁמָע
וַיִּכָּתֵב סֵפֶר זִכָּרוֹן לְפָנָיו לְיִרְאֵי יְיָ וּלְחֹשְׁבֵי שְׁמוֹ · אֵין
לִי אֶלָּא שְׁנַיִם · מִנַּיִן אֲפִילוּ אֶחָד שֶׁיּוֹשֵׁב וְעוֹסֵק בַּתּוֹרָה
שֶׁהַקָּדוֹשׁ בָּרוּךְ הוּא קוֹבֵעַ לוֹ שָׂכָר · שֶׁנֶּאֱמַר יֵשֵׁב בָּדָד
וְיִדּוֹם כִּי נָטַל עָלָיו: (ד) רַבִּי שִׁמְעוֹן אוֹמֵר · שְׁלֹשָׁה שֶׁאָכְלוּ
עַל שֻׁלְחָן אֶחָד וְלֹא אָמְרוּ עָלָיו דִּבְרֵי תוֹרָה כְּאִלּוּ אָכְלוּ
מִזִּבְחֵי מֵתִים · שֶׁנֶּאֱמַר כִּי כָּל־שֻׁלְחָנוֹת מָלְאוּ קִיא צֹאָה בְּלִי

"The parchment is being burnt, but the letters are soaring upward",
i.e. the Sacred Message written on it is indestructible.

the Divine Presence. Heb. *Shechinah*, the Holy Spirit that
makes God's presence felt by man. God's majesty descends upon a
group of two, three or ten persons engaged in sacred discourse. "How
many such majesties are there?" a heretic sneeringly asked of Rabban
Gamaliel II. He replied, "Does not the sun send forth a million rays
upon the earth? And should not the majesty of God, which is millions
of times brighter, be reflected in every spot on earth?"

though he sit alone. The Scriptural verse, removed from its context, is
made the basis of the fine thought; namely, that the Spirit of God abides
with the solitary man who allows his mind to dwell upon the holy
teachings of the Torah.

4. *Simeon. i.e.* R. Simeon ben Yochai (ca. 100–160).

A disciple of R. Akiba, and a most eminent Rabbi of his period. He
was a man of confident and independent mind; a hater of Roman
tyranny and a convinced democrat who declared, "Every Israelite is
to be regarded as of royal descent". In a wonderful parable, he
taught the solidarity of Israel. "In a boat at sea, one of the men began
to bore a hole in the bottom of the boat. On being remonstrated with,
he answered: 'I am only boring under my own seat.' 'Yes', said his
comrades, 'but when the sea rushes in, we shall all be drowned with
you'. So it is with Israel. Its weal or its woe is in the hands of every
individual Israelite". He spent many years in hiding from the Roman
authorities who had sentenced him to death. His life was adorned by
legend. He became the ideal of the Cabalists, and he was for many

together and interchange words of Torah, the Divine Presence
abides between them ; as it is said, Then they that feared the
Lord spake one with the other : and the Lord hearkened
and heard, and a book of remembrance was written before
him, for them that feared the Lord, and that thought upon
his Name. Now, the Scripture enables me to draw this inference in respect to two persons ; whence can it be deduced
that if even one person sedulously occupies himself with the
Torah, the Holy One, blessed be he, appoints unto him a
reward ? Because it is said, Though he sit alone, and meditate in stillness, yet he taketh it (the reward) upon him.

4. R. Simeon said, If three have eaten at a table and
have spoken there no words of Torah, it is as if they had
eaten of sacrifices to dead idols, of whom it is said, For all
their tables are full of vomit and filthiness ; the All-present

centuries held to be the author of the Zohar, which is deemed sacred by
the Cabalists. An annual festival is to this day celebrated by the
Mystics in his honour at Meron, in Northern Palestine. See also IV, 13.
    if three have eaten. Simeon ben Yochai expands the saying of R.
Chananya. In Judaism the meal is regarded as a religious service with
special benedictions before and after it. The act of eating is spiritualized
by being made subservient to the strengthening of the ties of domestic
affection and interest in higher things.
    spoken . . . no words of Torah. A company of three requires the
recital of Grace with a special responsive introduction. The Grace,
consisting of thanksgiving for food, coupled with historic and religious
memories, is in itself a fitting fulfilment of the demand for discourse
at table on sacred things.
    sacrifices to dead idols. If they paid no heed to religious matters,
and not even recited the Grace, the meal was merely for the satisfaction
of physical needs, with no sacredness whatever surrounding it. " Exag-
gerated statements such as this have the purpose of arresting the attention, and of driving home the lesson or the warning given " (Oesterley).
    vomit and filthiness. As his proof-text, R. Simeon chooses
Isaiah's denunciation of the drunkards of ancient Samaria, Chapter
28, in order to express his horror of the revels and feastings among
the Roman ruling classes. Such were often attended by indecency,
and the disgusting use of emetics in furtherance of gluttony. Not
such—taught R. Simeon—was to be the place of the meal and its
educational mission in the life of the Jew. The family table was to be
the family altar.

ג מָקוֹם · אֲבָל שְׁלֹשָׁה שֶׁאָכְלוּ עַל שֻׁלְחָן אֶחָד וְאָמְרוּ עָלָיו
דִּבְרֵי תוֹרָה כְּאִלּוּ אָכְלוּ מִשֻּׁלְחָנוֹ שֶׁל־מָקוֹם · שֶׁגֶּאֱמַר וַיְדַבֵּר
אֵלַי זֶה הַשֻּׁלְחָן אֲשֶׁר לִפְנֵי יְיָ : (ה) רַבִּי חֲנִינָא בֶּן־חֲכִינַי
אוֹמֵר · הַנֵּעוֹר בַּלַּיְלָה וְהַמְהַלֵּךְ בַּדֶּרֶךְ יְחִידִי וּמְפַנֶּה לִבּוֹ
לְבַטָּלָה הֲרֵי זֶה מִתְחַיֵּב בְּנַפְשׁוֹ : (ו) רַבִּי נְחוּנְיָא בֶּן־הַקָּנָה
אוֹמֵר · כָּל־הַמְקַבֵּל עָלָיו עֹל תּוֹרָה מַעֲבִירִים מִמֶּנּוּ עֹל
מַלְכוּת וְעֹל דֶּרֶךְ אֶרֶץ · וְכָל־הַפּוֹרֵק מִמֶּנּוּ עֹל תּוֹרָה נוֹתְנִים

the All-present is not (*in their thoughts*). lit. " without a place
(*makom*) "; but in Rabbinic Hebrew, *makom* is a synonym of God
(see on II, 14); hence the interpretation, " without the All-present ".

this is the table. Referring to the altar, which is said to have been
" three cubits high ", here taken as symbolical of three men seated at
the table. When the table is sanctified by prayer, and is not disgraced
by frivolity, it becomes holy like the altar.

5. *Chanina, the son of Chachinai.* A contemporary of R. Simeon
and disciple of R. Akiba; he lived during the first half of the second
century.

keeps awake at night. Even the waking hours due to sleeplessness
should be spent in serious meditation. " My soul is satisfied . . . when
I remember Thee upon my couch, and meditate on Thee in the night-
watches " (Psalm 63. 6f).

and who goes on his way alone. He is on a journey unaccompanied.
Having no companion with whom to discuss serious topics, there is
more danger of his mind dwelling upon frivolous matters.

turns his heart to idle thoughts. Idle thoughts lead to sin, therefore
the mind must be occupied with words of Torah; see Deuteronomy
VI, 7. " Thou shalt talk of them when thou sittest in thine house, and
when thou walkest by the way, and when thou liest down, and when
thou risest up." " This saying is one more illustration of that con-
secration of the whole of man's waking existence to the service of God,
which was for the Pharisee the ' way of the perfect life ' " (Herford).

sins against himself. Without the protective influence of Religion,
man is in constant danger of a lapse into evil, that might make him
incur guilt of the gravest nature.

6. *Nechunya, son of Ha-kana.* A contemporary of Rabban Yochanan. Later generations looked upon him as a foremost mystic. The
prayer, " We beseech thee ", recited after the Counting of the Omer, is
attributed to him. In his old age, he declared, " Never in my life have
I sought honour through the degradation of a colleague, nor has my
ill-will against any fellow-man lasted till night-time ".

III

5, 6

Sayings of the Fathers

is not (in their thoughts). But if three have eaten at a table and have spoken there words of Torah, it is as if they had eaten at the table of the All-present, to which the Scripture may be applied, And he said unto me, This is the table that is before the Lord.

5. R. Chanina, the son of Chachinai, said, He who keeps awake at night, and goes on his way alone, and turns his heart to idle thoughts, such a one sins against himself.

6. R. Nechunya, son of Ha-kana, said, Whoso receives upon himself the yoke of the Torah, from him the yoke of the kingdom and the yoke of worldly care will be removed ; but whoso casts off from him the yoke of the Torah, upon him will be laid the yoke of the kingdom and the yoke of worldly care.

yoke of the Torah. The multitude of commandments ordained by God is compared to a yoke (see p. 112), not as the symbol of oppression, but of obedience. Like the yoke harnessed to an animal, it provides guidance of right direction and useful service. " The Law will always be a yoke, though a glorious yoke ; and the duty of bending beneath it in humble and glad self-surrender is the characteristic obligation of Israel through the ages " (M. Joseph).

yoke of the kingdom. " Stands for the burdens, such as taxation put upon a man by the government under which he lives, or the oppression which he may suffer at the hands of the great " (Taylor).

worldly care. Heb. *derech eretz*, see on II, 2. The hardships, anxieties, and discontent in connection with the gaining of a livelihood.

will be removed. " Absorption in sacred study frees a man from care over worldly matters, and renders him invulnerable to the vicissitudes of time and fortune " (Derenbourg). The Tables of the Law are a charter of freedom ; see VI, 2. " To the man of true ethical and religious culture, civil law and the demands of society have ceased to be a burden ; to others, it is a yoke " (Geiger). In Büchler's opinion, R. Nechunya addressed himself not to all Jews, but to those who hesitated whether they should divide their time between the study of the Torah and a secular calling. Unlike R. Judah the Prince, who urged each scholar to have some worldly occupation, he advised them to make the study of the Torah their exclusive life-work. We have no evidence that either the Roman government remitted taxation in the case of scholars, or that the communities paid these and provided for their sustenance and that of their families.

casts off from him the yoke. A Heb. expression for rebellion. If a person seeks relief by revolt against God's commandments, the effect is to make the rigour of his mundane concerns more keenly felt.

ג

פרקי
אבות

עָלָיו עַל מַלְכוּת וְעַל דֶּרֶךְ אֶרֶץ : (ז) רַבִּי חֲלַפְתָּא בֶּן־
דּוֹסָא אִישׁ כְּפַר חֲנַנְיָא אוֹמֵר ּ עֲשָׂרָה שֶׁיּוֹשְׁבִים וְעוֹסְקִים
בַּתּוֹרָה שְׁכִינָה שְׁרוּיָה בֵינֵיהֶם ּ שֶׁנֶּאֱמַר אֱלֹהִים נִצָּב בַּעֲדַת־
אֵל ּ וּמִנַּיִן אֲפִילוּ חֲמִשָּׁה ּ שֶׁנֶּאֱמַר וַאֲגֻדָּתוֹ עַל־אֶרֶץ יְסָדָהּ ּ
וּמִנַּיִן אֲפִילוּ שְׁלֹשָׁה ּ שֶׁנֶּאֱמַר בְּקֶרֶב אֱלֹהִים יִשְׁפֹּט ּ וּמִנַּיִן
אֲפִילוּ שְׁנַיִם ּ שֶׁנֶּאֱמַר אָז נִדְבְּרוּ יִרְאֵי יְיָ אִישׁ אֶל־רֵעֵהוּ
וַיַּקְשֵׁב יְיָ וַיִּשְׁמָע ּ וּמִנַּיִן אֲפִילוּ אֶחָד ּ שֶׁנֶּאֱמַר בְּכָל־הַמָּקוֹם
אֲשֶׁר אַזְכִּיר אֶת־שְׁמִי אָבֹא אֵלֶיךָ וּבֵרַכְתִּיךָ : (ח) רַבִּי אֶלְעָזָר
אִישׁ בַּרְתּוֹתָא אוֹמֵר ּ תֶּן־לוֹ מִשֶּׁלּוֹ שָׁאַתָּה וְשֶׁלְּךָ שֶׁלּוֹ ּ
וְכֵן בְּדָוִד הוּא אוֹמֵר כִּי־מִמְּךָ הַכֹּל וּמִיָּדְךָ נָתַנּוּ לָךְ :
(ט) רַבִּי יַעֲקֹב אוֹמֵר ּ הַמְהַלֵּךְ בַּדֶּרֶךְ וְשׁוֹנֶה וּמַפְסִיק
מִמִּשְׁנָתוֹ וְאוֹמֵר מַה־נָּאֶה אִילָן זֶה מַה־נָּאֶה נִיר זֶה מַעֲלֶה

7. Chalafta, *the son of Dosa.* His saying continues the thought in mishna 3 and 4, and extends the number to a maximum of ten.

congregation. Heb. *edah,* the same word as in Numbers 14. 27, where it is used of the twelve spies, excluding Joshua and Caleb. This is the basis of the regulation which requires a minimum number (minyan) of ten adult males to constitute an *edah,* a "congregation", for public worship.

band. A collection of articles held together by the five fingers of the hand ; hence, the number five.

judges. The minimum number of judges to form a tribunal in Jewish Law is three.

I will come unto thee. The singular " thee " indicates one person.

8. *Elazar.* He was a disciple of R. Joshua ben Chananya, and a contemporary of R. Akiba.

Bertotha. In Galilee ; perhaps identical with Berothah (Ezekiel 47. 16).

give unto Him of what is His. An inspiring concept which ennobles life. All that man is and has, derives from God; body, soul, and life itself are what God has entrusted to him. They should consequently not be employed for self-advantage, but in His service. Rabbi Elazar himself faithfully practised his teaching. He was so generous in his gifts, that the official collectors of charity passed him by, for fear that he would contribute more than his means permitted.

7. R. Chalafta, the son of Dōsa, of the village of Chananya, said, When ten people sit together and occupy themselves with the Torah, the Shechinah abides among them, as it is said, God standeth in the congregation of the godly. And whence can it be shown that the same applies to five ? Because it is said, He hath founded his band upon the earth. And whence can it be shown that the same applies to three ? Because it is said, He judgeth among the judges. And whence can it be shown that the same applies to two ? Because it is said, Then they that feared the Lord spake one with the other ; and the Lord hearkened, and heard. And whence can it be shown that the same applies even to one ? Because it is said, In every place where I cause my Name to be remembered I will come unto thee and I will bless thee.

8. R. Elazar, of Bertotha, said, Give unto Him of what is His, seeing that thou and what thou hast are His : this 14 is also found expressed by David, who said, For all things come of Thee, and of Thine own we have given Thee.

9. R. Jacob said, He who is walking by the way and rehearses what he has learnt, and breaks off from his rehearsing and says, How fine is that tree, how fine is that field, him the Scripture regards as if he were guilty against himself.

9. *Jacob.* His father's name was Korshai. Some maintain that he was a grandson of Elisha ben Abuya (IV, 25) and a teacher of R. Judah the Prince. His saying states the duty of study of the Torah in extremest form. The Rabbis were certainly not indifferent to the beauty of Nature, as they prescribed various benedictions on beholding beautiful persons and things. Some of these blessings have been included in the Prayer Book.

breaks off. What is deprecated here is a wilful distraction of the mind from Torah-meditation by the surrounding scenery.

Scripture. No text is, or could well be, quoted, in support of the statement.

as if. Actually he does not sin, as the exclamation, " How fine is this tree ", is itself an adoration of God. It is only because learning is so much more important, that the breaking off therefrom deserves condemnation (Machzor Vitry and Tifereth Yisroel). This mishna has also been interpreted homiletically. " He who turns away from the

עָלָיו הַכָּתוּב כְּאִלּוּ מִתְחַיֵּב בְּנַפְשׁוֹ : (י) רַבִּי דוֹסְתַּאי בַּר
יַנַּאי מִשֵּׁם רַבִּי מֵאִיר אוֹמֵר · כָּל־הַשּׁוֹכֵחַ דָּבָר אֶחָד מִמִּשְׁנָתוֹ
מַעֲלֶה עָלָיו הַכָּתוּב כְּאִלּוּ מִתְחַיֵּב בְּנַפְשׁוֹ · שֶׁנֶּאֱמַר רַק
הִשָּׁמֶר לְךָ וּשְׁמֹר נַפְשְׁךָ מְאֹד פֶּן־תִּשְׁכַּח אֶת־הַדְּבָרִים
אֲשֶׁר־רָאוּ עֵינֶיךָ · יָכוֹל אֲפִילוּ תָּקְפָה עָלָיו מִשְׁנָתוֹ · תַּלְמוּד
לוֹמַר וּפֶן־יָסוּרוּ מִלְּבָבְךָ כֹּל יְמֵי חַיֶּיךָ · הָא אֵינוֹ מִתְחַיֵּב
בְּנַפְשׁוֹ עַד־שֶׁיֵּשֵׁב וִיסִירֵם מִלִּבּוֹ : (יא) רַבִּי חֲנִינָא בֶּן־דוֹסָא
אוֹמֵר · כֹּל שֶׁיִּרְאַת חֶטְאוֹ קוֹדֶמֶת לְחָכְמָתוֹ חָכְמָתוֹ
מִתְקַיֶּמֶת וְכֹל שֶׁחָכְמָתוֹ קוֹדֶמֶת לְיִרְאַת חֶטְאוֹ אֵין חָכְמָתוֹ
מִתְקַיֶּמֶת : (יב) הוּא הָיָה אוֹמֵר · כֹּל שֶׁמַּעֲשָׂיו מְרֻבִּים
מֵחָכְמָתוֹ חָכְמָתוֹ מִתְקַיֶּמֶת וְכֹל שֶׁחָכְמָתוֹ מְרֻבָּה מִמַּעֲשָׂיו
אֵין חָכְמָתוֹ מִתְקַיֶּמֶת : (יג) הוּא הָיָה אוֹמֵר · כֹּל שֶׁרוּחַ
הַבְּרִיּוֹת נוֹחָה הֵימֶנּוּ רוּחַ הַמָּקוֹם נוֹחָה הֵימֶנּוּ · וְכֹל שֶׁאֵין

Torah, *i.e.* gives up belief in Revelation, and seeks his religious inspiration from Nature, that man sins against his own soul " (J. H. Kara,
Soless l'minchah).

10. Dostai. An older contemporary of R. Judah the Prince, and
disciple of R. Meir.

whoso forgets. It is probable that this saying was not meant to have
a general application, but was intended for those who were styled
talmide chachamim, " disciples of the sages ". For such as these, forgetfulness was a serious defect; and highly culpable, if due to remissness on
their part.

now, one might suppose. This seems to be R. Dostai's comment on
R. Meir's statement.

too hard for him. Anyone may forget when what he tries to learn
is difficult.

of set purpose removes those lessons. This inference is drawn from the
words " all the days of thy life ". Unintentional forgetfulness can be
overcome by persistent study; but here we have a case where the
student deliberately abandons the study of the Torah. " A man should
be as careful to preserve his Torah as he is in regard to his money; for,
it is hardly gotten as gold, and perishes easily as glass. He who learns
Torah and does not *repeat* it, is as one who sows and does not reap." (Sifre).

[54]

10. R. Dostai, the son of Yannai, said in the name of R. Meir, Whoso forgets one word of his study, him the Scripture regards as if he had forfeited his life; for it is said, Only take heed to thyself, and keep thy soul diligently, lest thou forget the things which thine eyes have seen. Now, one might suppose that the same result follows even if a man's study has been too hard for him. To guard against such an inference, it is said, And lest they depart from thy mouth all the days of thy life. Thus, a person's guilt is not established until he deliberately and of set purpose removes those lessons from his heart.

11. R. Chaninà, the son of Dosa, said, He in whom the fear of sin comes before wisdom, his wisdom shall endure; but he in whom wisdom comes before the fear of sin, his wisdom will not endure.

12. He used to say, He whose deeds exceed his wisdom, his wisdom shall endure; but he whose wisdom exceeds his deeds, his wisdom will not endure.

13. He used to say, He in whom the spirit of his fellow-creatures takes delight, in him the Spirit of the All-present

11. *Chanina, the son of Dosa.* A disciple of Rabban Yochanan. Renowned as a mystic and wonder-worker. His sayings are amongst the simplest and sublimest in Aboth.

fear of sin. "A man with wisdom but without fear of Heaven, is like the man with the key of an inner court, but unable to enter because he has not the key of the outer court" (Talmud).

12. *he whose deeds exceed his wisdom.* Wisdom is only a means to an end; and, unless it fulfils itself in action of the right kind, it serves no true purpose and so cannot endure. It was a favourite saying of Raba (279–852): "The goal of wisdom is repentance and good deeds; so that a man shall not learn Torah, and study Mishna, and then contradict his father or master or teacher; as it is said, 'The fear of the Lord is the beginning of wisdom'". In the eyes of the Rabbis, the fear of the Lord was even more: it was the *whole* of wisdom; (i, 17).

13. *fellow-creatures.* Avoid doing things that even *appear* wrong, משום מראית עין. If a man so conducts himself as to win the approval of his fellows, he is assured of gaining the Divine approval. Such a statement does scant justice to the prophet, or the martyr: human favour does not, as a rule, shadow *them*. But R. Chanina was a mystic, and his deeper meaning is, when a man establishes harmonious

רוּחַ הַבְּרִיּוֹת נוֹחָה הֵימֶנּוּ אֵין רוּחַ הַמָּקוֹם נוֹחָה הֵימֶנּוּ:

(יד) רַבִּי דוֹסָא בֶּן־הָרְכִּינַס אוֹמֵר · שֵׁנָה שֶׁל־שַׁחֲרִית וְיַיִן

שֶׁל־צָהֳרַיִם וְשִׂיחַת הַיְלָדִים וִישִׁיבַת בָּתֵּי כְנֵסִיּוֹת שֶׁל־עַמֵּי

הָאָרֶץ מוֹצִיאִים אֶת־הָאָדָם מִן־הָעוֹלָם: (טו) רַבִּי אֶלְעָזָר

הַמּוֹדָעִי אוֹמֵר · הַמְחַלֵּל אֶת־הַקֳּדָשִׁים וְהַמְבַזֶּה אֶת־הַמּוֹעֲדוֹת

וְהַמַּלְבִּין פְּנֵי חֲבֵרוֹ בָּרַבִּים וְהַמֵּפֵר בְּרִיתוֹ שֶׁל־אַבְרָהָם

אָבִינוּ וְהַמְגַלֶּה פָנִים בַּתּוֹרָה שֶׁלֹּא כַהֲלָכָה אַף עַל פִּי שֶׁיֵּשׁ

בְּיָדוֹ תּוֹרָה וּמַעֲשִׂים טוֹבִים אֵין לוֹ חֵלֶק לָעוֹלָם הַבָּא:

(טז) רַבִּי יִשְׁמָעֵאל אוֹמֵר · הֱוֵי קַל לְרֹאשׁ וְנוֹחַ לְתִשְׁחֹרֶת

---

relations with his associates, any cause for displeasure on the part of
God is removed, and thus He too takes delight in him. Cf. I Samuel
2. 26 and Proverbs 3. 4.

14. *Dosa, the son of Horkinas.* A younger contemporary of Rabban
Yochanan. He was a man of wealth, and these warning words were
probably addressed to his social circle.

morning sleep. Involves the waste of precious hours of the day that
should be spent in work or study ; Proverbs 6. 9–11.

mid-day wine. Wine in Judaism is certainly not forbidden, when in
measure and in season. However, mid-day wine indisposes a man alike
for Torah and for business. " There are four stages from sobriety to
drunkenness. Before drinking, a man is innocent as a lamb; after
drinking enough, he is strong as a lion ; in the next stage, he is like a
hog ; when thoroughly drunken, he is like an ape, and dances and jests
and knows not what he is doing " (Midrash). Cf. Proverbs 23. 29–33.

children's talk. Or. " the babbling of youths ". A warning against
wasting too much time in listening to children's prattle, or to the idle
chatter of young people.

houses of assembly of the ignorant. See Psalm 1. 1. Frequenting
meeting-places of the vulgar, reduces a man to their level.

drive a man from the world. Cf. II, 16. The practices enumerated
render a man disinclined towards piety and the company of the learned.

15. *Elazar of Modim.* The home of the Maccabees. He was a
disciple of Rabban Yochanan, and was put to death by Bar Cochba,
having been falsely denounced by a Samaritan as a traitor. His saying
seems to have been directed against Gnostic and Jewish-Christian
sectarians in his day. Many of those " Liberal " Jews rejected all
religious authority, and their attitude opened the door to spiritual
nihilism. The Rabbis readily granted that some of these men may have
been well-meaning, men of considerable learning and social position;

[56]

III

14-16

Sayings of the Fathers

takes delight ; and he in whom the spirit of his fellow-creatures takes not delight, in him the Spirit of the All-present takes not delight.

14. R. Dosa, the son of Horkinas, said, Morning sleep and midday wine, and children's talk, and attending the houses of assembly of the ignorant, drive a man from the world.

15. R. Elazar of Modim said, He who profanes things sacred, and despises the festivals, and puts his fellow-man to shame in public, and makes void the covenant of Abraham our father, and makes the Torah bear a meaning other than the right, such a one, even though knowledge of the Torah and good deeds be his, has no share in the world to come.

16. R. Ishmael said, Be submissive to a superior, affable to a suppliant, and receive all men with cheerfulness.

but choosing to act as they did, they could not claim to be of the House of Israel.

things sacred. The saying is especially true when the words " things sacred " are taken in their larger, literal sense : he treats holy things as if they were not holy.

despises the festivals. By showing contempt for the Holy Occasions of the Jewish year, he not only violates the Divine commandment, but dissociates himself from Israel's history which is their background ; as well as from the community that finds its consciousness heightened by their celebration.

puts his fellow-man to shame in public. A heinous offence against the Golden Rule (II, 15). These sectarians " heckled " the Jewish teachers, and put them to shame at public discussions or gatherings (Moritz Friedländer).

makes void the covenant. Assimilationist Jews in ancient, as in modern, times sealed their apostasy by their repudiation of the Abrahamic covenant.

a meaning other than the right. A condemnation of arbitrary interpretations that are contrary to the accepted ruling.

though . . . Torah and good deeds be his. Although these are the highest qualifications a Jew can possess, they do not outweigh the serious offences enumerated. Those guilty of them cannot be considered as Israelites.

16. *Ishmael.* Grandson of a High Priest, he was taken captive to Rome after the fall of Jerusalem, and obtained his release through the efforts of R. Joshua ben Chananya; see also p. 37. His system of exegesis differed from that of Rabbi Akiba, and followed the plain meaning of

M

ג

נֶהֱוֶה מָקַבֵּל אֶת־כָּל־הָאָדָם בְּשִׂמְחָה : (יז) רַבִּי עֲקִיבָא
אוֹמֵר · שְׂחוֹק וְקַלּוּת רֹאשׁ מַרְגִּילִים אֶת־הָאָדָם לְעֶרְוָה :
מָסֹרֶת סְיָג לַתּוֹרָה מַעְשְׂרוֹת סְיָג לְעֹשֶׁר נְדָרִים סְיָג
לִפְרִישׁוּת סְיָג לַחָכְמָה שְׁתִיקָה : (יח) הוּא הָיָה אוֹמֵר ·
חָבִיב אָדָם שֶׁנִּבְרָא בְּצֶלֶם חִבָּה יְתֵרָה נוֹדַעַת לוֹ שֶׁנִּבְרָא
בְּצֶלֶם אֱלֹהִים · שֶׁנֶּאֱמַר כִּי בְּצֶלֶם אֱלֹהִים עָשָׂה אֶת־הָאָדָם :
חֲבִיבִים יִשְׂרָאֵל שֶׁנִּקְרְאוּ בָנִים לַמָּקוֹם חִבָּה יְתֵרָה נוֹדַעַת
לָהֶם שֶׁנִּקְרְאוּ בָנִים לַמָּקוֹם · שֶׁנֶּאֱמַר בָּנִים אַתֶּם לַיְיָ

פרקי
אבות

the Text. He was a lovable character. He is the author of the saying,
"The daughters of Israel are beautiful, but it is poverty which makes
them appear homely".

be submissive to a superior. lit. "be swift (to obey) a chief." Living
in a period when the hand of Rome was heavy upon the Jews, and her
local rulers were oppressors, he advised his brethren to accept in as
cheerful a spirit as possible the harsh conditions of their political
existence.

a suppliant. The meaning of the Heb. is uncertain. Some modern
authorities render: Be patient under forced service". Another
possible translation is; "Be deferential to your seniors, and affable to
your juniors".

receive all men with cheerfulness. A parallel to I, 15.

17-20. SAYINGS OF RABBI AKIBA.

17. *Akiba.* In the influence exerted by his teaching, Akiba (60–185)
is among the greatest intellectual forces in Israel. Tradition has it that he
was forty years old before he began the study of the Torah; and that he
had a romantic attachment to his wealthy employer's daughter, who,
despite all adversity, remained devoted to him. He joined Bar Cochba
in the Second War against the Romans, and met a martyr's death
about 185, on account of his determined stand for his Faith and People.
His principal teachers were Joshua ben Chananya and Eliezer ben
Hyrcanus. He held that the Torah was not written in the language
of every-day life. Not only every precept, but every word and letter
were meaning-laden, and not a dot was superfluous. His arrangement
of the Traditional laws was retained by his followers, Meir and Judah
the Prince, and is embodied in the Mishna.

Great in intellect, Akiba was no less great in character. In especial
he seems to have been conscious of the majesty of God and of His
supreme justice—a justice which, he declared, is yet altogether consistent

17. R. Akiba said, Jesting and levity lead a man on to lewdness. The Massorah is a fence to the Torah ; tithes are a fence to riches ; vows are a fence to abstinence ; a fence to wisdom is silence.

18. He used to say, Beloved is man, for he was created in the image of God ; but it was by a special love that it was made known to him that he was created in the image of God ; as it is said, For in the image of God made he man. Beloved are Israel, for they were called children of the All-present ; but it was by a special love that it was made

with goodness and mercy. "Whatever God doeth is for the best ", was his favourite saying. "That absolute submission to the will of God, which can perceive in suffering only an expression of God's fatherly love and mercy—*that* was the ideal of Akiba" (Schechter).

jesting and levity. Judaism does not denounce merriment as such, and a jester may leave the saintly behind in true merit of life. R. Akiba's saying warns against jesting that leads to undue familiarity between the sexes. In the sphere of religion and morality, "fences" are necessary safeguards against falling into sin.

Massorah. i.e. "tradition" (see on 1, 1). The term is used particularly of the traditional transmission of the Scriptural text, which preserved the Divine Revelation from falsification through accident, ignorance or sectarian bias.

tithes are a fence to riches. Allocating to religious and charitable purposes the ordained portion, does not reduce a man's wealth. It makes the owner conscious that his property is due to a Divine Providence (mishna 8), and this feeling saves him from squandering his possessions unwisely.

vows. A vow serves to keep him who makes it from doing what he might ignorantly or carelessly do without it. Though many have found vows helpful in cultivating self-restraint and shunning over-indulgence, Scripture discourages vowing. See "Vows and Vowing in Judaism," *Numbers*, 810 (Soncino, 780).

abstinence. Heb. *perishuth*, lit. "separation" from what defiles the body or contaminates the soul. The term "pharisee" is by some scholars derived from this word.

silence. See on 1, 17.

18. *man.* The human being, without limitation of creed and racial origin.

by a special love. It is with God as with man. To declare one's love is a more signal proof of affection than love without such declaration. Divine possibilities have been implanted in man ; but it is an especial mark of God's love to His human children that they have been endowed with the *consciousness* of these Divine possibilities within them.

אֱלֹהֵיכֶם : חֲבִיבִים יִשְׂרָאֵל שֶׁנִתַּן לָהֶם כְּלִי חֶמְדָּה חִבָּה

יְתֵרָה נוֹדַעַת לָהֶם שֶׁנִתַּן לָהֶם כְּלִי חֶמְדָּה שֶׁבּוֹ נִבְרָא

הָעוֹלָם · שֶׁנֶּאֱמַר כִּי לֶקַח טוֹב נָתַתִּי לָכֶם תּוֹרָתִי אַל-תַּעֲזֹבוּ :

(יט) הַכֹּל צָפוּי וְהָרְשׁוּת נְתוּנָה וּבְטוֹב הָעוֹלָם נָדוֹן וְהַכֹּל

לְפִי רֹב הַמַּעֲשֶׂה : (כ) הוּא הָיָה אוֹמֵר · הַכֹּל נָתוּן בְּעֵרָבוֹן

וּמְצוּדָה פְרוּשָׂה עַל-כָּל-הַחַיִּים · הֶחָנוּת פְּתוּחָה וְהַחֶנְוָנִי

מַקִּיף וְהַפִּנְקָס פָּתוּחַ וְהַיָד כּוֹתֶבֶת וְכָל הָרוֹצֶה לִלְווֹת יָבֹא

beloved are Israel. The Selection of Israel is a great world-historic event. Even greater is the fact, that his high calling has been made known to Israel. It is his Jewish Consciousness that lends immortality to the Jew.

children unto the Lord. Every Israelite is a son of God, and he approaches his Heavenly Father in a spirit of child-like trust.

desirable instrument. The Torah, whose commandments are " more to be desired than gold " (Psalm 19. 11) and are of eternal validity.

through which the world was created. The Rabbis held that the Torah existed before the universe, and contained the spiritual design according to which the world was created. " Wisdom," in the Book of Proverbs, is identified with the Torah in such passages as : " The Lord by wisdom founded the earth " (8. 19). In this manner, the Rabbis gave expression to the profound truth that the Creation serves an eternal, spiritual purpose.

19. This saying of Rabbi Akiba is among the most important in Aboth, and lays down a fundamental doctrine of practical religion. Despite the fact that God foresees the course which a man will adopt when faced with the choice of two paths, man has free choice. God's foreknowledge and the freedom of man's will are reconcilable ; so are God's mercy and justice in His dealings with man.

everything is foreseen. Everything past, present and future is seen by God, even as a watchman in a lighthouse tower sees ships in the distance coming and going, and can in a tempest foresee which among them must dash itself to destruction.

by grace. lit. " with goodness ". The Psalmist's declaration, " The Lord is good to all, and His tender mercies are over all His works " (Psalm 145. 9), is a favourite text of the Rabbis. They underline the word " all ", and deduce from it that His goodness extends to animals as well as man (see p. 87), to the Gentile as well as to the Israelite. Akiba's universalist note is probably derived from his teacher Rabbi Joshua ben Chananya.

yet all is according to the amount of work. God is good and merciful, 　**[60]**

known to them that they were called children of the All-present; as it is said, Ye are children unto the Lord your God. Beloved are Israel, for unto them was given the desirable instrument ; but it was by a special love that it was made known to them that that desirable instrument was theirs, through which the world was created; as it is said, For I give you good doctrine ; forsake ye not my Law.

19. Everything is foreseen, yet freedom of choice is given ; and the world is judged by grace, yet all is according to the amount of work.

20. He used to say, Everything is given on pledge, and a net is spread for all the living : the shop is open ; and the dealer gives credit ; and the ledger lies open ; and the hand writes ; and whosoever wishes to borrow may come and borrow; but the collectors regularly make their daily round; and exact payment from man, whether he be content or not ;

but He rewards or punishes according to man's doings on earth.

20. *given on pledge.* The doctrine previously stated is now given in language taken from commerce. The world is likened to the office of a merchant.

everything. *i.e.* life and all its opportunities are granted to man on the " pledge " that he will utilize them wisely and well.

a net is spread for all the living. Nobody can evade his responsibility for the use he makes of his life, because all are called to account before the Divine Tribunal.

the shop is open. The world is stocked with what God has provided for the welfare and happiness of His creatures.

the dealer gives credit. God does not demand immediate payment ; after death will be the reckoning.

and the hand writes. There is a record of every obligation incurred, expressing the thought of II, 1, "All thy deeds are written in a Book ". Jewish folklore declares that every night, while the body is asleep, the soul ascends on high, and records whatever sin and transgression had been committed during the day.

whosoever wishes to borrow. Man makes free use of his share of the world's goods, and adapts it to his wishes.

their daily round. But man is under supervision, and the manner in which he disposes of God's bounty is examined. If that bounty has been abused, His agents exact penalties, such as calamity and suffering.

whether he be content or not. " With his knowledge or without his knowledge " ; *i.e.* whether he is conscious or not that the troubles which befall him are a visitation for his misuse of life.

וְיִלְוֶה וְהַגַּבָּאִים מַחֲזִירִים תָּדִיר בְּכָל־יוֹם וְנִפְרָעִים מִן־הָאָדָם
מִדַּעְתּוֹ וְשֶׁלֹּא מִדַּעְתּוֹ וְיֵשׁ לָהֶם עַל מַה־שֶּׁיִּסְמֹכוּ וְהַדִּין
דִּין אֱמֶת · וְהַכֹּל מְתֻקָּן לַסְּעוּדָה: (כא) רַבִּי אֶלְעָזָר בֶּן־
עֲזַרְיָה אוֹמֵר · אִם אֵין תּוֹרָה אֵין דֶּרֶךְ אֶרֶץ אִם אֵין דֶּרֶךְ
אֶרֶץ אֵין תּוֹרָה · אִם אֵין חָכְמָה אֵין יִרְאָה אִם אֵין יִרְאָה
אֵין חָכְמָה · אִם אֵין דַּעַת אֵין בִּינָה אִם אֵין בִּינָה אֵין
דַּעַת · אִם אֵין קֶמַח אֵין תּוֹרָה אִם אֵין תּוֹרָה אֵין קֶמַח :
(כב) הוּא הָיָה אוֹמֵר · כֹּל שֶׁחָכְמָתוֹ מְרֻבָּה מִמַּעֲשָׂיו לְמָה
הוּא דוֹמֶה · לְאִילָן שֶׁעֲנָפָיו מְרֻבִּים וְשָׁרָשָׁיו מֻעָטִים וְהָרוּחַ
בָּאָה וְעוֹקַרְתּוֹ וְהוֹפַכְתּוֹ עַל פָּנָיו · שֶׁנֶּאֱמַר וְהָיָה כְּעַרְעָר

they have that whereon they can rely. The judgment is a judgment of
truth. The penalty is a just one, determined by the person's actions.
"This affirmation of the absolute justice of God is one of the
unshakable foundations of the Jewish religion throughout its history."
(Herford).

everything is prepared for the feast. If a man made use of his opportunities, he is destined to participate in "Thy goodness which Thou
hast laid up for them that fear Thee" (Psalm 31. 20). But even the
sinner may, after repentance, or retribution at the hands of Heaven,
join the "banquet". The figure of a banquet for the happiness of the
righteous in the Hereafter is, of course, pure symbolism; and the
details in regard to the feast—*e.g.* Leviathan—are folk-lore. Rabh
(160-247), the renowned pupil of Rabbi Judah the Prince, declared, "In
the World to come, there is neither eating nor drinking nor marrying;
no envy, emulation or strife; but the righteous sit, with crowns on
their heads, and feast on the splendour of the Divine Presence."

21. *Elazar, the son of Azaryah.* He lived from 70 to 135. Succeeded
Rabban Gamaliel II as the Nasi of the Jabneh Sanhedrin, when the
latter was deposed. On the restoration of Gamaliel to office, Elazar
became Av Beth-Din. He came from an ancient family and was a man
of wealth. He accompanied Joshua ben Chananya and Akiba on their
mission to Rome—One of his noble sayings—that has become authoritative in Judaism—is : "Only sins against God does the Day of Atonement remove. Sins against man are not forgiven, unless the offended
party has first been reconciled".

[62]

and they have that whereon they can rely in their demand ; and the judgment is a judgment of truth ; and everything is prepared for the feast.

21. R. Élazar, the son of Azaryah, said, Where there is no Torah, there are no manners ; where there are no manners, there is no Torah : where there is no wisdom, there is no fear of God ; where there is no fear of God, there is no wisdom : where there is no knowledge, there is no understanding ; where there is no understanding, there is no knowledge : where there is no meal, there is no Torah ; where there is no Torah, there is no meal.

22. He used to say, He whose wisdom exceeds his deeds, to what is he like ? To a tree whose branches are many, but whose roots are few ; and the wind comes and plucks it up and overturns it upon its face; as it is said, And he shall be like a lonely juniper tree in the desert, and shall not see when good cometh ; but shall inhabit the parched places in the wilderness, a salt land and not inhabited. But he whose

---

no Torah . . . no manners. *Derech eretz*, here translated "manners ", means " practical life ". Without Religion, such practical life is the existence of a heathen or an animal, degraded from its true meaning and dignity.

no manners . . . no Torah. Without practical life and in the absence of social relationship, religious learning is futile piety, instead of a living, beneficent influence.

no fear of God . . . no wisdom. Moral insensibility and religious nihilism are in Scripture the marks of the "fool".

no knowledge . . . no understanding. Without knowledge, the faculty of understanding is left with nothing on which to work.

no understanding . . . no knowledge. Knowledge is the accumulation of data, and is sterile without the " understanding " which enables it to be applied.

no meal . . . no Torah. Unless the body is adequately nourished, the brain will not function properly, and study will be ineffective.

no Torah . . . no meal. Man's duty is to feed his mind and spirit, as well as his body. " Man doth not live by bread alone, but by every thing that proceedeth out of the mouth of the Lord doth man live " (Deuteronomy 8. 3).

22. *He whose wisdom exceeds his deeds.* R. Elazar takes up the saying of R. Chanina ben Dosa (mishna 12), and illustrates it with the aid of Biblical texts.

בְּעֶרְכָּה וְלֹא יִרְאֶה פְּי-יָבוֹא טוֹב וְשָׁכַן חֲרֵרִים בַּמִּדְבָּר אֶרֶץ

מְלֵחָה וְלֹא תֵשֵׁב · אֲבָל כֹּל שֶׁמַּעֲשָׂיו מְרֻבִּים מֵחָכְמָתוֹ

לְמָה הוּא דוֹמֶה · לְאִילָן שֶׁעֲנָפָיו מְעָטִים וְשָׁרָשָׁיו מְרֻבִּים

שֶׁאֲפִילוּ כָּל-הָרוּחוֹת שֶׁבָּעוֹלָם בָּאוֹת וְנוֹשְׁבוֹת בּוֹ אֵין מְזִיזִים

אוֹתוֹ מִמְּקוֹמוֹ · שֶׁנֶּאֱמַר וְהָיָה כְּעֵץ שָׁתוּל עַל-מַיִם וְעַל-יוּבַל

יְשַׁלַּח שָׁרָשָׁיו וְלֹא יִרְאֶה כְּי-יָבֹא חֹם וְהָיָה עָלֵהוּ רַעֲנָן

וּבִשְׁנַת בַּצֹּרֶת לֹא יִדְאָג וְלֹא יָמִישׁ מֵעֲשׂוֹת פֶּרִי : (כג) רַבִּי

אֶלְעָזָר חִסְמָא אוֹמֵר · קִנִּין וּפִתְחֵי נִדָּה הֵן הֵן גּוּפֵי

הֲלָכוֹת · תְּקוּפוֹת וְגִמַטְרִיָּאוֹת פַּרְפְּרָיוֹת לַחָכְמָה :

רַבִּי חֲנַנְיָא בֶּן-עֲקַשְׁיָא וכו׳

פֶּרֶק רְבִיעִי :

כָּל-יִשְׂרָאֵל וכו׳

(א) בֶּן-זוֹמָא אוֹמֵר · אֵיזֶהוּ חָכָם · הַלּוֹמֵד מִכָּל-אָדָם ·

23. *Elazar Chisma.* A disciple of R. Joshua ben Chananya and R. Akiba. He was renowned for his knowledge of astronomy.

laws concerning the sacrifice of birds. Heb. *kinnin*, the name of a Mishna tractate dealing with the Biblical regulations concerning the offering of birds in circumstances enumerated in Leviticus, chapters 12, 13 and 15.

purification of women. Heb. *niddah*, also the name of a tractate expounding the laws of Leviticus 15. 19f.

ordinances of moment. i.e. essential laws of Judaism. These two are specified because, superficially considered, they would appear to be subjects of minor importance. They are, however, ordinances of the Torah, and as such deserving of close study.

[64]

IV

1

Sayings of the Fathers

deeds exceed his wisdom, to what is he like ? To a tree whose branches are few, but whose roots are many, so that even if all the winds in the world come and blow upon it, it cannot be stirred from its place; as it is said, And he shall be as a tree planted by the waters ; and that spreadeth out its roots by the river, and shall not perceive when heat cometh, but his leaf shall be green ; and shall not be troubled in the year of drought, neither shall cease from yielding fruit.

23. R. Elazar Chisma said, The laws concerning the sacrifices of birds and the purification of women are ordinances of moment ; astronomy and geometry are the after-courses of wisdom.

"Rabbi Chananya," etc., p. 27.

CHAPTER IV

"All Israel," etc., p. 1 ɔ .

1. Ben Zoma said, Who is wise ? He who learns from all men ; as it is said, From all my teachers I have gotten

---

astronomy. lit. " revolutions " of the heavenly bodies. Astronomical knowledge was held in high esteem by the Rabbis. Bar Kappara, a friend of Rabbi Judah the Prince, declared, " He who knows how to compute the course of the sun and the revolution of the planets and neglects to do so, of him Scripture says, ' They regard not the work of the Lord, neither consider the operation of His hands ' " (Isaiah 5. 12).

geometry. The Heb. is a transliteration of the Greek word from which *geometry* is derived. Here it means mathematics in general. " Gematria " also denotes an arithmetical method of exegesis, in which the numerical values of the Hebrew letters in a word are taken into account. Thus, " Satan has no power on the Day of Atonement, because the numerical value of the letters in השטן is only 364 ".

after-courses of wisdom. Important as these studies are, it is the Torah which is the beginning and the foundation of Jewish education. They are the auxiliaries to Wisdom, which is Torah.

CHAPTER IV.

SAYINGS OF YOUNGER CONTEMPORARIES OF RABBI AKIBA.

1. *Ben Zoma.* Simeon ben Zoma, a disciple of R. Joshua ben Chananya. He—together with Ben Azzai, Elisha ben Abuya and Akiba—was attracted by the theosophic speculation of the Gnostics concerning

פרקי
אבות

שֶׁנֶּאֱמַר מִכָּל־מְלַמְּדַי הִשְׂכַּלְתִּי : אֵיזֶהוּ גִבּוֹר · הַכּוֹבֵשׁ אֶת־
יִצְרוֹ · שֶׁנֶּאֱמַר טוֹב אֶרֶךְ אַפַּיִם מִגִּבּוֹר וּמשֵׁל בְּרוּחוֹ מִלֹּכֵד
עִיר : אֵיזֶהוּ עָשִׁיר · הַשָּׂמֵחַ בְּחֶלְקוֹ · שֶׁנֶּאֱמַר יְגִיעַ כַּפֶּיךָ
כִּי תֹאכֵל אַשְׁרֶיךָ וְטוֹב לָךְ · אַשְׁרֶיךָ בָּעוֹלָם הַזֶּה וְטוֹב
לָךְ לָעוֹלָם הַבָּא : אֵיזֶהוּ מְכֻבָּד · הַמְכַבֵּד אֶת־הַבְּרִיּוֹת ·
שֶׁנֶּאֱמַר כִּי מְכַבְּדַי אֲכַבֵּד וּבֹזַי יֵקָלּוּ : (ב) בֶּן־עַזַּי אוֹמֵר ·
הֱוֵי רָץ לְמִצְוָה קַלָּה וּבוֹרֵחַ מִן־הָעֲבֵרָה · שֶׁמִּצְוָה גּוֹרֶרֶת

the nature of the Godhead, the process of Creation and the mystery of
Evil. Many lost their way in that jungle of heretical thinking. Ben
Zoma and Ben Azzai died young, in consequence of their assiduous
devotion to those studies ; Elisha ben Abuya became estranged from
Judaism ; and Akiba alone emerged in peace, to become a giant of
religious loyalty and leadership in the annals of Judaism. Ben Zoma's
four questions and answers, sublime in their simplicity, are among
the most noteworthy gnomic sayings in religious literature.

he who learns from all men. The wise man has an open mind, and is
willing to learn from anybody. The proof-texts seem to be later editorial
additions.

he who subdues his passions. lit. " his *yetzer* ", his evil inclination ;
see on II, 16, also p. 25. Self-conquest is the highest form of strength.
The story of Samson, who is strong physically but weak morally, and
suffers shipwreck through following " the desire of the eyes ", is the
type of deep tragedy.

Another noble definition of " mighty " given by the Rabbis is, " he
who turns his enemy into a friend ".

he who rejoices in his portion. The Heb. idiom for " he who is content ". The words may also be rendered, " he who is happy in his
portion ". Only where there is *happiness* in one's life-work is the greatest
good achieved for self as for others. Rabbi Elimelech, one of the
Chassidic teachers, declared : " Whatever a man's occupation, the
wares in which he deals, or the work he performs ; so long as he respects
his wares, honours his calling and is happy in his work—they will be a
source of sanctification to him, and of usefulness to his fellow-men ".

he who respects his fellow-men. lit. " his fellow-creatures (beriyyoth)",
see on I, 12. This is one of the world's great sayings : it is the key to all
worthy living and beneficent influence in one's human circle. Like
his colleague Ben Azzai, Ben Zoma preached the Brotherhood of man.
And he did this by emphasizing the *interdependence* of men : " not a
mouthful did Adam taste before he ploughed and sowed, cut and bound
the sheaves, threshed and winnowed the grain, ground and sifted the
flour, kneaded the dough and baked it into bread ; but I get up in the

IV

2

Sayings of the Fathers

understanding. Who is mighty? He who subdues his passions; as it is said, He that is slow to anger is better than the mighty, and he that ruleth over his spirit than he that taketh a city. Who is rich? He who rejoices in his portion; as it is said, When thou eatest the labour of thine hands, happy art thou, and it shall be well with thee: happy art thou—in this world; and it shall be well with thee—in the world to come. Who is worthy of honour? He who respects his fellow-men; as it is said, For them that honour me I will honour, and they that despise me shall be held in contempt.

2. Ben Azzai said, Run to do even a slight precept, and flee from transgression; for one good deed draws another

morning, and find all this ready before me". The web of the social organism was to him more than a mark of civilization; it was the basis of practical religion, of the ethical requirement to honour our fellow-creatures.

2. Ben Azzai. Simeon ben Azzai; according to one tradition, he was martyred with Rabbi Akiba by the Romans in the year 135. Extraordinary assiduity and piety rendered him an outstanding character among the scholars that gathered round Rabban Yochanan ben Zakkai at Yavneh. His name ought to be known to every student of Religion. He is the author of the great saying, *The reward of virtue is virtue, and the wages of sin is sin*; *i.e.* one good deed leads to another good deed, and the greatest punishment of evil-doing is that it leads to further evil-doing. He was a renowned exegete, and it was due to his decisive voice that the books of Ecclesiastes and Song of Songs were included in the canon of Scripture (Yadayim III, 5). His was a new conception of the Golden Rule. When Rabbi Akiba, in the spirit of Hillel, declared "Thou shalt love thy neighbour as thyself" (Leviticus 19. 18) to be the great principle in Religion, Ben Azzai maintained that even of more fundamental importance was the opening verse of the fifth chapter of Genesis—"This is the book of the generations of man . . . in the image of God made He him". For it taught first, the unity of mankind, not merely as members of one race or one people, but as created in the image of God; and, secondly, it proclaimed, because of its God-likeness, the infinite worth of each and every human soul.

run. Show eagerness to perform even a "slight precept", the same term as in II, 1; but the reason here given is quite different. The performance of even a slight duty renders easier the performance of the next, possibly heavier, duty.

good deed. Heb. *mitzvah*, commandment; in later Hebrew, any good deed is so termed.

flee from transgression. As one should run *to* a good deed, so he should run *from* a transgression, and remove himself from temptation;

[67]

מִצְוָה וַעֲבֵרָה גּוֹרֶרֶת עֲבֵרָה שֶׁשְּׂכַר מִצְוָה מִצְוָה וּשְׂכַר
עֲבֵרָה עֲבֵרָה : (נ) הוּא הָיָה אוֹמֵר · אַל־תְּהִי בָז לְכָל־אָדָם
וְאַל־תְּהִי מַפְלִיג לְכָל־דָּבָר שֶׁאֵין לְךָ אָדָם שֶׁאֵין לוֹ שָׁעָה
וְאֵין לְךָ דָּבָר שֶׁאֵין לוֹ מָקוֹם : (ד) רַבִּי לְוִיטַס אִישׁ יַבְנֶה
אוֹמֵר · מְאֹד מְאֹד הֱוֵי שְׁפַל רוּחַ שֶׁתִּקְוַת אֱנוֹשׁ רִמָּה :
(ה) רַבִּי יוֹחָנָן בֶּן־בְּרוֹקָה אוֹמֵר · כָּל־הַמְחַלֵּל שֵׁם שָׁמַיִם
בַּסֵּתֶר נִפְרָעִים מִמֶּנּוּ בַּגָּלוּי · אֶחָד בְּשׁוֹגֵג וְאֶחָד בְּמֵזִיד
בְּחִלּוּל הַשֵּׁם : (ו) רַבִּי יִשְׁמָעֵאל בְּנוֹ אוֹמֵר · הַלּוֹמֵד עַל־

because each wrongful act dulls the conscience, so that there is weaker
moral resistance to the commission of a second offence. The Rabbis
explain the opening verse of the Psalms as follows : "He who first *walks*
in the counsel of the wicked ", next " *stands* in the way of sinners ", and
at length " *sits* in the seat of scoffers ".

one good deed draws another good deed in its train. And so the good
life is the result. " The good deed itself is its own complete reward "
(Philo). Various philosophers (*e.g.* Spinoza) have quoted and utilized
this great saying of Ben Azzai, without mentioning the source.

wages of sin is sin. The human tragedy of sin consists not so much
in its punishment as in its progeny. One lie immediately entails another
lie to bolster it up, and one crime calls forth a second and a third crime
to hide it from the eyes of men.

" This is the curse of every evil deed,
That it begets a further deed of shame."

Furthermore, every evil action leaves in our characters the tendency to
commit the same action again. And the predisposition to commit the
sin of which we are guilty, does not stop with our lives. *Our vices may
reappear in those that come after us, unto the third and fourth generation.*

3. *despise not any man.* All men are equally God's creatures; and the
honest toil of the humblest menial is a contribution to the social order.
In the words of the Rabbis of Yavneh : " I am a creature of God, and
my neighbour is also His creature ; my work is in the city, and his in
the field ; I rise early to my work, and he rises early to his. As he
cannot excel in my work, so I cannot excel in his work. But perhaps
thou sayest, ' I do great things, and he small things ! ' We have learnt
that it matters not whether one does much or little, if only he direct his
heart to Heaven." " In God's sight it is not the nature of a man's work
nor its intrinsic importance that counts, but the whole-heartedness of the
thought of God with which it is done " (Moore).

good deed in its train, and one sin, another sin ; for the reward of a good deed is a good deed, and the wages of sin is sin.

3. He used to say, Despise not any man, and carp not at any thing ; for there is not a man that has not his hour, and there is not a thing that has not its place.

4. R. Levitas, of Yavneh, said, Be exceedingly lowly of spirit, since the hope of man is but the worm.

5. R. Yochanan, the son of Berokah, said, Whosoever profanes the Name of Heaven in secret, will suffer the penalty for it in public ; and this, whether the Heavenly Name be profaned in ignorance or in wilfulness.

6. R. Ishmael, his son, said, He who learns in order to

---

carp not at anything. This is part of the folk-wisdom of the peoples ; *e.g.* the prince who carps at cobwebs, and in the end is saved by such cobweb when hiding in the hollow of a tree from his mortal enemies. This is told of David when fleeing from Saul, many centuries before Robert Bruce became the hero of a similar legend.

his hour . . . place. Every person or object is sure at some time and in some circumstances to be reckoned with, either for good or for evil (Israelstam).

4. *Levitas.* A contemporary of R. Akiba. Little is known of him.

exceedingly lowly of spirit. Like mishna 24, in which Samuel the Younger took two verses from Proverbs as his motto, Rabbi Levitas' warning seems to be a quotation from Ecclesiasticus 7. 17. " Humble altogether thy pride, for man's expectation is worms ". Though not included in the canon, that book (in Hebrew, " The Wisdom of Joshua ben Sira ") is several times quoted in Rabbinical literature as if it were Scripture.

5. *Yochanan, the son of Berokah.* A disciple of R. Joshua ben Chananya.

profanes the name of Heaven. See on i, 11.

in secret. He secretly commits a crime that tarnishes the honour of his Faith and the good name of Israel. Sooner or later, his deed will be exposed, and his true character revealed to the men whose esteem he is anxious to possess.

in ignorance or in wilfulness. Profanation of the Name remains an unforgivable sin, whether the act is unintentional or due to malignity. But the degree of punishment will not be the same, since one is immeasurably more culpable than the other.

6. *Ishmael, his son.* Lived in the latter half of the second century. In his opinion, learning alone is of little value, unless it leads to teaching, and above all else to practice.

he who learns. The Jew is the eternal learner, who is daily to extend

מְנָת לְלַמֵּד מַסְפִּיקִים בְּיָדוֹ לִלְמוֹד וּלְלַמֵּד · וְהַלּוֹמֵד עַל־

מְנָת לַעֲשׂוֹת מַסְפִּיקִים בְּיָדוֹ לִלְמוֹד וּלְלַמֵּד לִשְׁמוֹר

וְלַעֲשׂוֹת : (ז) רַבִּי צָדוֹק אוֹמֵר · אַל־תִּפְרוֹשׁ מִן־הַצִּבּוּר

וְאַל־תַּעַשׂ עַצְמְךָ כְּעוֹרְכֵי הַדַּיָּנִים וְאַל־תַּעֲשֶׂהָ עֲטָרָה

לְהִתְגַּדֶּל־בָּהּ וְלֹא קַרְדֹּם לַחְפָּר־בָּהּ · וְכַךְ הָיָה הִלֵּל אוֹמֵר ·

וְדאִשְׁתַּמַּשׁ בְּתָגָא חֲלָף · הָא לָמַדְתָּ כָּל־הַנֶּהֱנֶה מִדִּבְרֵי

תוֹרָה נוֹטֵל חַיָּיו מִן־הָעוֹלָם : (ח) רַבִּי יוֹסֵי אוֹמֵר · כָּל־

הַמְכַבֵּד אֶת־הַתּוֹרָה גּוּפוֹ מְכֻבָּד עַל־הַבְּרִיּוֹת · וְכָל־הַמְחַלֵּל

אֶת־הַתּוֹרָה גּוּפוֹ מְחֻלָּל עַל־הַבְּרִיּוֹת : (ט) רַבִּי יִשְׁמָעֵאל

פרקי
אבות
ד

his knowledge of Torah, the guide to conduct; his mastery of Hebrew, the language of Religion; and his understanding of the everlasting truths enshrined in Israel's Scriptures.

in order to teach. The most sacred task of every Jew is to teach the high and holy truths of Judaism to those who are under his influence.

Heaven will grant him the opportunity. i.e. he is given adequate powers.

in order to practise. The true ultimate purpose of all study; I, 17.

to observe. The Heb. term is often used in connection with negative commandments. It may also be translated, "to defend". He will share in the defence of Judaism against enemies whether from within or without; II, 19.

and to practise. Which is the fruit of learning, and the test of the sincerity of the learner. "Whosoever learns Torah and does not practise it, it were better for him never to have been born" (Midrash).

7. Zadok. Yochanan ben Zakkai successfully interceded for his life with the Romans before the fall of Jerusalem.

separate not thyself. A verbal repetition of Hillel's saying (II, 5); and the next clause is also a repetition of Judah ben Tabbai's saying (I, 8). Some texts omit both, but the remainder of the paragraph is also based on a quotation. These sayings of the eminent Sages who had preceded him, appealed to R. Zadok so strongly that he took them as his motto.

crown. The object of study must not be the desire to receive the deference accorded to scholars. Rabbi Tarfon passing through a garden, ate some figs that had been left behind. The custodians of the garden came up and beat him. When he called out who he was, they let him go. All his days he grieved over this: "Woe is me, for I have used the crown of the Torah for my own benefit".

[70]

teach, Heaven will grant him the opportunity both to learn -
and to teach ; but he who learns in order to practise,
Heaven will grant him the opportunity to learn and to
teach, to observe and to practise.

7. R. Zadok said, Separate not thyself from the congregation ; (in the judge's office) act on the counsel's part ;
make not of the Torah a crown wherewith to aggrandize
thyself, nor a spade wherewith to dig. So also used Hillel
to say, He who makes a worldly use of the crown of the
Torah shall pass away. Hence thou mayest infer, that
whosoever derives a profit for himself from the words of the
Torah is helping on his own destruction.

8. R. José said, Whoso honours the Torah will himself
be honoured by mankind, but whoso dishonours the Torah
will himself be dishonoured by mankind.

9. R. Ishmael, his son, said, He who shuns the judicial

nor a spade wherewith to dig. Nor may study of the Torah be turned
into a means of support. Neither the Prophets nor the Rabbis accepted
payment for their instruction. It was only with the rise of new economic
conditions towards the close of the Middle Ages, that Jewish teachers
could no longer maintain the old rule of free teaching. Simon ben
Zemach Duran (1861–1444)—physician, rabbinical authority and
philosopher—was the first rabbi to accept a salary from his congregation
in Algiers. In explaining this mishna in his commentary on Aboth, he
relates that he had lost all his possessions in the pogrom at Majorca ;
that in a Moorish environment he could not derive subsistence from his
medical skill; and that a return to European lands was impossible
for him, as he was in danger of his life at the hands of the Inquisition.
so also used Hillel to say. See I, 18.
is helping on his own destruction. lit. " removes his life from the
world ". The Torah is a " tree of life " only to them who lay hold of it
from love, not to those who pursue their self-interest by its means.
8. *José.* Son of Chalafta. One of the most distinguished of R. Akiba's
disciples.
honours the Torah. He reveres the Teaching revealed therein, and
accepts it as a guide of life. Such a one—R. José maintains—will command the esteem of fellow-Jews and all fellow-men who respect the
consecrated life.
whoso dishonours the Torah. By violating its teachings, his standard
of life will become debased, and men will despise him.
9. *Ishmael, his son.* Lived in the latter half of the second century
of the Christian era.

בְּנוֹ אוֹמֵר · הַחוֹשֵׂךְ עַצְמוֹ מִן־הַדִּין פּוֹרֵק מִמֶּנּוּ אֵיבָה וְגָזֵל
וּשְׁבוּעַת שָׁוְא · וְהַגַּס לִבּוֹ בְּהוֹרָאָה שׁוֹטֶה רָשָׁע וְגַס רוּחַ:

(י) הוּא הָיָה אוֹמֵר · אַל־תְּהִי דָן יְחִידִי שֶׁאֵין דָּן יְחִידִי
אֶלָּא אֶחָד · וְאַל־תֹּאמַר קַבְּלוּ דַעְתִּי שֶׁהֵם רַשָּׁאִים וְלֹא אָתָּה:

(יא) רַבִּי יוֹנָתָן אוֹמֵר · כָּל־הַמְקַיֵּם אֶת־הַתּוֹרָה מֵעֹנִי סוֹפוֹ
לְקַיְּמָהּ מֵעשֶׁר · וְכָל־הַמְבַטֵּל אֶת־הַתּוֹרָה מֵעשֶׁר סוֹפוֹ לְבַטְּלָהּ
מֵעֹנִי : (יב) רַבִּי מֵאִיר אוֹמֵר · הֱוֵי מְמַעֵט בְּעֵסֶק וַעֲסֹק
בַּתּוֹרָה וֶהֱוֵי שְׁפַל־רוּחַ בִּפְנֵי כָל־אָדָם · וְאִם־בָּטַלְתָּ מִן־הַתּוֹרָה
יֶשׁ־לְךָ בְּטֵלִים הַרְבֵּה כְּנֶגְדֶּךָ · וְאִם־עָמַלְתָּ בַתּוֹרָה יֶשׁ־לוֹ

he who shuns the judicial office. So translated, the saying is advice
against the acceptance of judgeship, since it is a thankless task. The
Hebrew is lit. " he who withholds himself from (pronouncing) judgment " ; and this may mean a judge who is disinclined to give a verdict,
and proposes a settlement by compromise.

hatred. By the losing party, either towards the judge or the other
litigant. In a compromise, the loss is only partial, and therefore the
resentment less deep.

robbery. In the event of the judge passing a wrong judgment, he
robs the man of what is his.

vain swearing. Litigation often involves the taking of an oath. This
is something sacred, and should only be taken when altogether un-
avoidable. A compromise would obviate this procedure.

but he who presumptuously lays down decisions. lit, "he who
accustoms himself to lay down decisions". If it refers to a judge, it is a
condemnation of arrogance. He should be possessed of a spirit of
humility and responsibility. The word for "decision" is commonly
used of the answer to a question on religious law (shaalah) given by a
Rabbi. He, too, when discharging that duty must be humble.

foolish. Over-confidence in a judge may lead to disastrous results.
" Seest thou a man wise in his own eyes ? There is more hope of a fool
than of him " (Proverbs 26. 12).

wicked. Acting in a haughty spirit, he may be guilty of gross injustice as a judge.

of an arrogant spirit. A vice which the Rabbis frequently censured ;
see III, 1 ; IV, 4. " Whoever has an arrogant spirit, the Holy One, [72]

office rids himself of hatred, robbery and vain swearing ;
but he who presumptuously lays down decisions is foolish,
wicked and of an arrogant spirit. .

10. He used to say, Judge not alone, for none may judge
alone save One ; neither say (to thy judicial colleagues),
Accept my view, for the choice is theirs (to concur) ; and it
is not for thee (to compel concurrence).

11. R. Jonathan said, Whoso fulfils the Torah in the
midst of poverty, shall in the end fulfil it in the midst of
wealth ; and whoso neglects the Torah in the midst of
wealth, shall in the end neglect it in the midst of poverty.

12. R. Meir said, Lessen thy toil for worldly goods, and
be busy in the Torah ; be humble of spirit before all men ;
if thou neglectest the Torah, many causes for neglecting it
will present themselves to thee, but if thou labourest in the
Torah, He has abundant recompense to give thee.

blessed be He, says of him, ' I and he cannot dwell in the world together ' " (Talmud).

10. *judge not alone.* As pointed out on III, 7, at least three judges
were required to try a case. Jewish Law, however, allowed a suit in-
volving property to be adjudicated by only one, if he was a judicial
expert ; but this practice is not recommended by R. Ishmael, because
the responsibility is too heavy.

One. God.

for the choice is theirs. The two judges have the right to express their
opinion, and the third judge must follow the majority.

11. *Jonathan.* His father's name was Joseph, and he was a disciple
of R. Akiba and R. Ishmael ben Elisha.

in the midst of wealth. He neglects his religious duties to devote
himself to the care of his possessions. Even in poverty, such a one will
find no time for Torah. In either of the two cases mentioned, what is
begun in youth is not likely to be altered in age.

12. *Meir.* The most famous of R. Akiba's disciples ; see on VI, 1.

lessen thy toil for worldly goods. Cf. Hillel's saying in II, 6.

humble of spirit. It is remarkable how often the virtue of humility
is advocated in Aboth. It is characteristic of Rabbinic teaching.

if thou neglectest. As soon as a person has broken the regular routine
of study, he will find many pretexts for further neglect. " Forsake the
Torah a single day, and it will forsake thee two days " (Talmud).

abundant recompense. Cf. II, 19, 21.

ד
פרקי
אבות

שָׂכָר הַרְבֵּה לְתֵּן־לָהּ : (יג) רַבִּי אֱלִיעֶזֶר בֶּן־יַעֲקֹב אוֹמֵר ·
הָעוֹשֶׂה מִצְוָה אַחַת קוֹנֶה לוֹ פְּרַקְלִיט אֶחָד · וְהָעוֹבֵר עֲבֵרָה
אַחַת קוֹנֶה לוֹ קַטֵּגוֹר אֶחָד · תְּשׁוּבָה וּמַעֲשִׂים טוֹבִים
כִּתְרֵיס בִּפְנֵי הַפֻּרְעָנוּת : (יד) רַבִּי יוֹחָנָן הַסַּנְדְּלָר אוֹמֵר ·
כָּל־כְּנֵסִיָּה שֶׁהִיא לְשֵׁם שָׁמַיִם סוֹפָהּ לְהִתְקַיֵּם · וְשֶׁאֵינָהּ לְשֵׁם
שָׁמַיִם אֵין סוֹפָהּ לְהִתְקַיֵּם : (טו) רַבִּי אֶלְעָזָר בֶּן־שַׁמּוּעַ
אוֹמֵר · יְהִי כְבוֹד תַּלְמִידָךְ חָבִיב עָלֶיךָ כְּשֶׁלָּךְ וּכְבוֹד
חֲבֵרָךְ כְּמוֹרָא רַבָּךְ וּמוֹרָא רַבָּךְ כְּמוֹרָא שָׁמָיִם : (טז) רַבִּי
יְהוּדָה אוֹמֵר · הֱוֵי זָהִיר בְּתַלְמוּד שֶׁשִּׁגְגַת תַּלְמוּד עוֹלָה

13. *Eliezer, the son of Jacob.* Disciple of R. Akiba.

advocate . . . accuser. Before the judgment-throne of God when a man's life is being assessed. Each act of religious loyalty pleads in his favour ; each act of disloyalty tells against him.

repentance. In Jewish teaching, repentance is the sole, but inexorable, condition of God's forgiveness and the restoration of His favour ; and the Divine forgiveness and favour are never refused to genuine repentance. Countless are the Rabbinic sayings on repentance. " It was created before the universe, because without it the world could not endure. Great is repentance, for it brings healing to the world. Great is repentance, for it reaches to the Throne of God. There is nothing greater than repentance ". See introductory notes to New Year and the Day of Atonement.

deeds of charity. Proof of the sincerity of repentance. The Rabbis dwell specially on the text, " And God saw their works, that they turned from their evil way ; and God relented of the evil, which He said He would do unto them ; and He did it not " (Jonah 3. 10)—not their fasting and sackcloth, but their " works ", *i.e.* good deeds, secured their pardon.

14. *Yochanan, the sandal maker.* Born in Alexandria. He was a disciple of R. Akiba.

every assembly. It may be a general reflection like that of v, 20. Modern commentators assert that it was suggested by prevailing conditions of the day. After the defeat of Bar Cochba in the year 135, most of the communities were ruined, and had to be reconstructed. The task was of overwhelming difficulty ; and R. Yochanan

IV

13-16

*Sayings
of the
Fathers*

13. R. Eliezer, the son of Jacob, said, He who does one good deed has gotten himself one advocate; and he who commits one transgression has gotten himself one accuser. Repentance and deeds of charity are as a shield against punishment.

14. R. Yochanan, the sandal maker, said, Every assembly which is in the name of Heaven will in the end be established, but that which is not in the name of Heaven will not in the end be established.

15. R. Elazar, the son of Shammua, said, Let the honour of thy disciple be as dear to thee as thine own, and the honour of thine associate be like the reverence for thy master, and the reverence for thy master like the fear of Heaven.

16. R. Judah said, Be cautious in teaching, for an error in teaching may amount to presumptuous sin.

taught that so long as the effort was made " in the name of Heaven ", the results would be enduring. God does not allow wholly to fail what is done for His sake.

15. *Elazar, the son of Shammua.* Disciple of R. Akiba and colleague of R. Meir.

honour of thy disciple. The duty of respect from the pupil to the master occurs several times in Aboth; here the teacher is bidden equally to esteem his disciple who is devoting himself to study.

associate. i.e. colleague.

reverence for thy master like the fear of Heaven. A much misunderstood clause. It does not mean that the teacher is made equal to God. It means, "that there was a reverence due to the teacher of Torah (by reason of the sacredness of the Torah) and a reverence due to God, the Giver of the Torah; and that to pay that reverence was an equal obligation in each case " (Herford).

16. *Judah.* The son of Ilai; a disciple of R. Akiba and a teacher of great distinction.

presumptuous sin. Although the teacher may have erred unintentionally, the effect may be so serious in spreading false doctrine, that his guilt is equal to the commission of an intentional sin. To cause others to do wrong, the Rabbis emphasized, was much worse than himself to do wrong.

ד

פרקי
אבות

זָדוֹן : (יז) רַבִּי שִׁמְעוֹן אוֹמֵר · שְׁלֹשָׁה כְתָרִים הֵן · כֶּתֶר תּוֹרָה

וְכֶתֶר כְּהֻנָּה וְכֶתֶר מַלְכוּת · וְכֶתֶר שֵׁם טוֹב עוֹלֶה עַל

גַּבֵּיהֶן : (יח) רַבִּי נְהוֹרַי אוֹמֵר · הֱוֵה גוֹלֶה לִמְקוֹם תּוֹרָה

וְאַל־תֹּאמַר שֶׁהִיא תָבוֹא אַחֲרֶיךָ · שֶׁחֲבֵרֶיךָ יְקַיְּמוּהָ בְיָדֶךָ ·

וְאֶל־בִּינָתְךָ אַל־תִּשָּׁעֵן : (יט) רַבִּי יַנַּאי אוֹמֵר · אֵין בְּיָדֵינוּ

לֹא מִשַּׁלְוַת הָרְשָׁעִים וְאַף לֹא מִיִּסּוּרֵי הַצַּדִּיקִים : (כ) רַבִּי

מַתִּתְיָה בֶּן־חָרָשׁ אוֹמֵר · הֱוֵה מַקְדִּים בִּשְׁלוֹם כָּל־אָדָם ·

וֶהֱוֵה זָנָב לָאֲרָיוֹת וְאַל־תְּהִי רֹאשׁ לַשּׁוּעָלִים : (כא) רַבִּי יַעֲקֹב

אוֹמֵר · הָעוֹלָם הַזֶּה דּוֹמֶה לִפְרוֹזְדוֹר בִּפְנֵי הָעוֹלָם הַבָּא ·

17. *Simeon.* Ben Yochai, see on III, 4. His saying is among the very greatest in Aboth.

crowns. Symbols of dignity.

learning. lit. " Torah ", religious learning.

crown of priesthood. Scripture states, " Thou shalt set the mitre upon his (Aaron's) head, and put the holy crown upon the mitre " (Exodus 29. 6).

a good name. Cf. " a good name is rather to be chosen than great riches " (Proverbs 23. 1) and, " A good name is better than precious oil " (Ecclesiastes 7. 1).

excels them all. Because it alone is the tribute paid to personality and character. " A man attains to priesthood and royalty by heredity, and even learning is not invariably accompanied by nobility of character. Only in the case of a bearer of a good name, do we find outward honour combined with inner worth " (G. Beer).

18. *Rabbi Nehorai.* A name given to several Rabbis. In this instance it is said to be a pseudonym of R. Elazar ben Arach (II, 10).

a home of the Torah. A place where eminent teachers reside, so that one may benefit from their instruction ; see VI, 9.

the Torah will come after thee. If the author is R. Elazar ben Arach, he may have had his own experience in mind. On the death of his teacher, Rabban Yochanan, he left his associates and lived in Emmaus which was not " a home of the Torah ", and he forgot his learning. To the Jew of to-day, this mishna is a warning to live in, or near, a Jewish community.

for there thy associates. True knowledge is the result of contact with other minds ; see I, 16.

upon thine own understanding. To unravel difficulties in one's studies, instead of resorting to guidance from a competent teacher.

IV

17-21

Sayings of the Fathers

17. R. Simeon said, There are three crowns : the crown of learning, the crown of priesthood, and the crown of royalty ; but the crown of a good name excels them all.

18. R. Nehorai said, Wander forth to a home of the Torah—and say not that the Torah will come after Thee—for there thy associates will establish thee in the possession of it ; and lean not upon thine own understanding.

19. R. Yannaï said, It is not in our power to explain either the prosperity of the wicked or the afflictions of the righteous.

20. R. Mattithya, the son of Cheresh, said, Be beforehand in the salutation of peace to all men ; and be rather a tail to lions than a head to foxes.

21. R. Jacob said, This world is like an ante-chamber to the world to come ; prepare thyself in the ante-chamber, that thou mayest enter into the hall.

Your own unguided mind may lead to error, heresy, apostasy. The words, "lean not upon thine understanding", are a quotation from Proverbs 3. 5.

19. *Yannai.* His identity is uncertain. He may be the father of R. Dostai in III, 10 ; if so, he was a contemporary of R. Meir.

it is not in our power to explain. Man can answer neither the question, Why do the wicked flourish ? nor, Why do the righteous suffer ? "This saying may be an explanatory comment on the words from Proverbs with which the last mishna closes" (Hoffmann). It might also be translated, "There is not in our hands the security of the wicked, nor the chastisements of the righteous". This would then describe the political status of the Jews in the days of the author : neither hopelessly bad nor wholly good (Graetz).

20. *Mattithya, the son of Cheresh.* A disciple of R. Eliezer, who fled from the Holy Land after the defeat of Bar Cochba, and lived in Rome.

beforehand in the salutation. A counsel of prudence, especially to a Jew in an unfriendly environment.

be rather a tail to lions. Evidently formulated in opposition to a proverb current both in Rome and Palestine : "Better be a head of foxes, than a tail among lions ".

21. *Jacob.* See III, 9.

prepare thyself. For life in the Hereafter, by good actions and repentance for misdeeds. "Prepare to meet thy God, O Israel " (Amos 4. 12).

the hall. The Heb. is a transliteration of a Greek word for a dining

הַתְקֵן עַצְמְךָ בִּפְרוֹזְדוֹר כְּדֵי שֶׁתִּכָּנֵס לִטְרַקְלִין : (כב) הוּא
הָיָה אוֹמֵר · יָפָה שָׁעָה אַחַת בִּתְשׁוּבָה וּמַעֲשִׂים טוֹבִים
בָּעוֹלָם הַזֶּה מִכָּל־חַיֵּי הָעוֹלָם הַבָּא · וְיָפָה שָׁעָה אַחַת שֶׁל־
קֹרַת רוּחַ בָּעוֹלָם הַבָּא מִכָּל־חַיֵּי הָעוֹלָם הַזֶּה : (כג) רַבִּי
שִׁמְעוֹן בֶּן־אֶלְעָזָר אוֹמֵר · אַל־תְּרַצֶּה אֶת־חֲבֵרְךָ בְּשָׁעַת
כַּעְסוֹ וְאַל־תְּנַחֲמֶנּוּ בְּשָׁעָה שֶׁמֵּתוֹ מֻטָּל לְפָנָיו וְאַל־תִּשְׁאַל
לוֹ בִּשְׁעַת נִדְרוֹ וְאַל־תִּשְׁתַּדֵּל לִרְאוֹתוֹ בִּשְׁעַת קַלְקָלָתוֹ :
(כד) שְׁמוּאֵל הַקָּטָן אוֹמֵר · בִּנְפֹל אוֹיִבְךָ אַל־תִּשְׂמָח וּבִכָּשְׁלוֹ
אַל־יָגֵל לִבֶּךָ · פֶּן־יִרְאֶה יְיָ וְרַע בְּעֵינָיו וְהֵשִׁיב מֵעָלָיו אַפּוֹ :
(כה) אֱלִישָׁע בֶּן־אֲבוּיָה אוֹמֵר · הַלּוֹמֵד יֶלֶד לְמָה הוּא דוֹמֶה ·

hall, and may have been chosen because the happiness of the World to come is conceived under the image of a banquet (III, 20).

22. *better is one hour.* " This mishna is one of the noblest pearls in the whole realm of religious proverb-lore. Its first half rests on the contrast between this life and the Hereafter. This life is the world of toil and sowing ; the Hereafter the world of reaping and reward. There-fore, this life is the superior. For the happiness experienced in perform-ing good deeds, exceeds the joy felt in the reward offered for those good deeds " (Beer). In the midst of time and mortality, the per-formance of good deeds bestows eternal life and everlasting happiness.

blissfulness of spirit. In life upon earth, man is engaged in a continuous struggle between his higher and lower self. Even if his better nature gains the mastery, he feels the strain of the contest, and must be ever watchful to maintain the victory. In the Hereafter, the struggle is over, and he enjoys a tranquility which is impossible in his lifetime (A. Cohen).

23. *Simeon, the son of Elazar.* A disciple of R. Meir. Advises utmost tact in approaching a man under a strain. His saying proves him to have been a man endowed with exceptional delicacy of feeling, combined with knowledge of human nature. Another of his notable sayings is : " If the young tell thee, Build, and the old tell thee, Destroy, follow the counsel of the elders ; for the destruction of the elders is construction, and the construction of the young is destruc-tion ".

do not appease. Do not try to pacify him while his anger is hot. Your interference might only render his fury more uncontrollable.

IV

22-25

Sayings of the Fathers

22. He used to say, Better is one hour of repentance and good deeds in this world than the whole life of the world to come ; yet better is one hour of blissfulness of spirit in the world to come than the whole life of this world.

23. R. Simeon, the son of Elazar, said, Do not appease thy fellow in the hour of his anger, and comfort him not in the hour when his dead lies before him, and question him not in the hour of his vow, and strive not to see him in the hour of his disgrace.

24. Samuel the Younger used to quote, Rejoice not when thine enemy falleth, and let not thine heart be glad when he stumbleth : lest the Lord see it and it displease him, and he turn away his wrath from him [unto thee].

25. Elisha, the son of Abuya, said, If one learns as a

when his dead lies before him. His grief is then so poignant that silence is the greatest kindness. According to Jewish custom, condoling with the mourner begins *after* the burial.

in the hour of his vow. A man makes a vow under the stress of emotion ; and, if he is questioned on its extent at the time it is made, he may only commit himself more deeply.

in the hour of his disgrace. Do not force yourself upon him in the hour of his humiliation.

24. *Samuel the Younger.* He lived in the first century, at Jabneh. He is the author of the Twelfth Benediction (" against heretics ") in the Amidah; see p. 148.

used to quote. lit. "says", but his saying consists only of two Biblical verses (Proverbs 24. 17, 18). Among the sins solemnly repudiated in Job 31. 29 (" If I rejoiced at the destruction of him that hated me, or exulted when evil found him ") is joy at the misfortune of an enemy. Like Job, Samuel the Younger ranks rejoicing over your enemy's woes as a grave sin. Some commentators connect Samuel's favourite verses with the last mishna. To force your presence upon a person in the hour of his disgrace, is like gloating over his misfortune. Others take his citation as a warning to the Jews, when they rejoiced over a set-back to their enemies during the revolt against Rome (I. H. Weiss).

25. *Elisha, the son of Abuya.* The Faust of Talmudic literature. Despite his learning, he broke away from Judaism, and became "Acher", *i.e.* another man. Rabbi Meir, his one time disciple, remained his friend throughout life. It was probably due to this friendship that Elisha's words were admitted into Aboth. Indeed, it is missing in some Prayer Books.

לְדְיוֹ כְּתוּבָה עַל־נְיָר חָדָשׁ ׃ וְהַלּוֹמֵד זָקֵן לְמָה הוּא דוֹמֶה ׃
לְדְיוֹ כְּתוּבָה עַל־נְיָר מָחוּק ׃ (כו) רַבִּי יוֹסֵי בַּר יְהוּדָה אִישׁ
כְּפַר הַבַּבְלִי אוֹמֵר ׃ הַלּוֹמֵד מִן־הַקְּטַנִּים לְמָה הוּא דוֹמֶה ׃
לְאוֹכֵל עֲנָבִים קֵהוֹת וְשׁוֹתֶה יַיִן מִגִּתּוֹ ׃ וְהַלּוֹמֵד מִן־הַזְּקֵנִים
לְמָה הוּא דוֹמֶה ׃ לְאוֹכֵל עֲנָבִים בְּשׁוּלוֹת וְשׁוֹתֶה יַיִן יָשָׁן ׃
(כז) רַבִּי מֵאִיר אוֹמֵר ׃ אַל־תִּסְתַּכֵּל בְּקַנְקַן אֶלָּא בְּמַה שֶּׁיֶּשׁ
בּוֹ ׃ יֵשׁ קַנְקַן חָדָשׁ מָלֵא יָשָׁן וְיָשָׁן שֶׁאֲפִילוּ חָדָשׁ אֵין בּוֹ ׃
(כח) רַבִּי אֶלְעָזָר הַקַּפָּר אוֹמֵר ׃ הַקִּנְאָה וְהַתַּאֲוָה וְהַכָּבוֹד
מוֹצִיאִים אֶת־הָאָדָם מִן הָעוֹלָם ׃ (כט) הוּא הָיָה אוֹמֵר ׃
הַיְּלוֹדִים לָמוּת וְהַמֵּתִים לְהֵחָיוֹת וְהַחַיִּים לָדוֹן לֵידַע

clean paper. lit. " new paper ". What is written upon it remains clearly legible. The mind is similarly fresh to receive impressions in youth.

blotted paper. lit. " rubbed paper ". The material was the papyrus leaf. Owing to its costliness, it was sometimes used more than once, the writing being rubbed out with stone. The new writing was not clear, because the original script remained, faintly visible. In like manner, new instruction in old age leaves a blurred impression on the mind. Therefore, the study of Torah should begin in youth. Obviously, this saying dates from before Ben Abuya's fall.

26. *José, the son of Judah of Kephar Babli.* A disciple of R. Elazar ben Shammua (mishna 15) and older contemporary of R. Judah the Prince.

unripe grapes. Which set the teeth on edge.

wine from the vat. The wine is not matured, and leads to intoxication. In like manner, the teaching by the young is liable to be immature, inexact, and leading to error.

old wine. Which is a source of health and festive joy. A simile for ripe knowledge, which only the experience of years can supply.

27. *Meir.* See on VI, 1. Some manuscripts omit " Meir ", and the author is then " Rabbi ", *i.e.* R. Judah the Prince. He disagreed with the preceding dictum. The age of a teacher is no criterion of the soundness and value of his scholarship. Unripeness in judgment is not the exclusive possession of the young ; nor is wisdom, of the old.

child, what is it like ? Like ink written on clean paper. If one learns as an old man, what is it like ? Like ink written on blotted paper.

26. R. José, the son of Judah, of Kephar Babli, said, He who learns from the young, to what is he like ? To one who eats unripe grapes, or drinks wine from the vat. And he who learns from the old, to what is he like ? To one who eats ripe grapes, or drinks old wine.

27. R. Meir said, Look not at the flask, but at what it contains : there may be a new flask full of old wine, and an old flask that has not even new wine in it.

28. R. Elazar Ha-kappar said, Envy, desire and ambition drive a man out of the world.

29. He used to say, They that are born are destined to die ; and the dead to be brought to life again ; and the living to be judged, to know, to make known, and to be made conscious that he is God, he the Maker, he the Creator,

28. *Elazar Ha-kappar.* An associate of R. Judah the Prince. " Kappar " may mean, " the man from Cyprus ".

envy. This is distinct from emulation, which increases skill and wisdom.

desire. Unbridled hankering after pleasure.

ambition. lit. " lust of honour ". Three anti-social qualities are enumerated which are a hindrance to harmonious relations with our fellow-men ; cf. II, 16.

drive a man . . . world. " They break the ties which should unite a man to his fellow-man ; and, whether or not they lead to physical death, they destroy his higher life as a moral being, made in the likeness of God " (Herford).

29. A meditation on Human Destiny and the Judgment Day.

the dead to be brought to life again. The clear teaching of the Rabbis, in opposition to contemporary schools of thought that denied the Resurrection. It was their firm conviction that " if what never before existed, exists ; why cannot that which once existed, exist again ? " See p. 255.

and the living. i.e. Those who have been brought to life again.

to know . . . made conscious. i.e. that one may know from others, that one may make others know, and that one may know of himself. " Truths which in this world men are *taught,* will in the world to come be known without a teacher " (Taylor).

the Maker. lit. " the Fashioner ".

וּלְהוֹדִיעַ וּלְהִנָּדַע שֶׁהוּא אֵל הוּא הַיּוֹצֵר הוּא הַבּוֹרֵא הוּא הַמֵּבִין הוּא הַדַּיָּן הוּא הָעֵד הוּא בַּעַל דִּין הוּא עָתִיד לָדוּן בָּרוּךְ הוּא שֶׁאֵין לְפָנָיו לֹא עַוְלָה וְלֹא שִׁכְחָה וְלֹא מַשּׂוֹא פָנִים וְלֹא מִקַּח שֹׁחַד · וְדַע שֶׁהַכֹּל לְפִי הַחֶשְׁבּוֹן · וְאַל־ יַבְטִיחֲךָ יִצְרְךָ שֶׁהַשְּׁאוֹל בֵּית מָנוֹס לָךְ · שֶׁעַל כָּרְחֲךָ אַתָּה נוֹצָר וְעַל כָּרְחֲךָ אַתָּה נוֹלָד וְעַל כָּרְחֲךָ אַתָּה חַי וְעַל כָּרְחֲךָ אַתָּה מֵת וְעַל כָּרְחֲךָ אַתָּה עָתִיד לִתֵּן דִּין וְחֶשְׁבּוֹן לִפְנֵי מֶלֶךְ מַלְכֵי הַמְּלָכִים הַקָּדוֹשׁ בָּרוּךְ הוּא :

רַבִּי חֲנַנְיָא בֶּן־עֲקַשְׁיָא וכו׳

פֶּרֶק חֲמִישִׁי :

כָּל־יִשְׂרָאֵל וכו׳

(א) בַּעֲשָׂרָה מַאֲמָרוֹת נִבְרָא הָעוֹלָם · וּמַה־תַּלְמוּד לוֹמַר וַהֲלֹא בְּמַאֲמָר אֶחָד יָכוֹל לְהִבָּרְאוֹת· אֶלָּא לְהִפָּרַע מִן־ הָרְשָׁעִים שֶׁמְּאַבְּדִים אֶת־הָעוֹלָם שֶׁנִּבְרָא בַּעֲשָׂרָה מַאֲמָרוֹת

---

the Complainant. Heb. *baal-din*; opposite of the defendant.

taking of bribes. Cf. II Chronicles 19. 7. The medieval commentators explain that no unrepented misdeed will be overlooked, because of good actions.

respect of persons. Partiality.

everything is according to the reckoning. Continues the thought of the preceding clause. Cf. III, 19 and 20.

imagination. i.e. " thy (evil) inclination "; see II, 16. It overcomes scruples by suggesting that wrong can be done with impunity; but there is no escape from the justice of God.

a place of refuge. In the belief that there is no Hereafter.

perforce thou wilt die. No person can escape death which is the forerunner of the Judgment.

to give account and reckoning. As in III, 1. This solemn admonition fittingly concludes the chapter, with which possibly the whole of Aboth at one time closed.

V

1

Sayings of the Fathers

he the Discerner, he the Judge, he the Witness, he the Complainant ; he it is that will in future judge, blessed be he, with whom there is no unrighteousness, nor forgetfulness, nor respect of persons, nor taking of bribes : know also that everything is according to the reckoning : and let not thy imagination give thee hope that the grave will be a place of refuge for thee ; for perforce thou wast formed, and perforce thou wast born, and thou livest perforce, and perforce thou wilt die, and perforce thou wilt in the future have to give account and reckoning before the Supreme King of kings, the Holy One, blessed be he.

" R. Chananya," etc., p. 27.

CHAPTER V

" All Israel," etc., p. 13 .

1. With ten Sayings the world was created. What does this teach us ? Could it not have been created with one Saying ? It is to make known the punishment that will befall the wicked who destroy the world that was created

CHAPTER V.

ANONYMOUS AND NUMBER-SAYINGS.

The sayings in this chapter are nearly all of them anonymous. In form, they consist of a series of groups of ten, seven, four and three things. In substance, they touch upon cosmogony, speculation, sacred history, and the varieties of men, minds and motives. While the preceding chapters are predominantly ethical, this chapter is largely haggadah, folk-lore.

1–18. Number-Groups.
The idea of tabulating things according to number, is found as early as, *e.g.*, Isaiah 17. 6, Amos 1. 8 and Proverbs 6. 16. In oral teaching, number-schemes are a valuable aid to memory.

1–9. Groups of ten.
1. The importance of God's work of Creation i enhanced by the fact that it was created by ten sayings, instead of one single fiat. This is evidence—humanly speaking—of continuous and careful planning in Creation and its marvels. Great, therefore, is the merit of those who by their lives help to maintain the moral nature of that Creation ; and terrible is the responsibility of those who would destroy it.

וְלִתֵּן שָׂכָר טוֹב לַצַּדִּיקִים שֶׁמְּקַיְּמִים אֶת־הָעוֹלָם שֶׁנִּבְרָא
בַּעֲשָׂרָה מַאֲמָרוֹת : (ב) עֲשָׂרָה דוֹרוֹת מֵאָדָם וְעַד נֹחַ
לְהוֹדִיעַ כַּמָּה אֶרֶךְ אַפַּיִם לְפָנָיו ' שֶׁכָּל־הַדּוֹרוֹת הָיוּ מַכְעִיסִים
לְפָנָיו עַד שֶׁהֵבִיא עֲלֵיהֶם אֶת־מֵי הַמַּבּוּל : (ג) עֲשָׂרָה
דוֹרוֹת מִנֹּחַ וְעַד אַבְרָהָם לְהוֹדִיעַ כַּמָּה אֶרֶךְ אַפַּיִם לְפָנָיו '
שֶׁכָּל־הַדּוֹרוֹת הָיוּ מַכְעִיסִים לְפָנָיו עַד שֶׁבָּא אַבְרָהָם אָבִינוּ
וְקִבֵּל שָׂכָר כֻּלָּם : (ד) עֲשָׂרָה נִסְיוֹנוֹת נִתְנַסָּה אַבְרָהָם
אָבִינוּ וְעָמַד בְּכֻלָּם לְהוֹדִיעַ כַּמָּה חִבָּתוֹ שֶׁל־אַבְרָהָם אָבִינוּ :
(ה) עֲשָׂרָה נִסִּים נַעֲשׂוּ לַאֲבוֹתֵינוּ בְּמִצְרָיִם וַעֲשָׂרָה עַל
הַיָּם : (ו) עֶשֶׂר מַכּוֹת הֵבִיא הַקָּדוֹשׁ בָּרוּךְ הוּא עַל
הַמִּצְרִיִּים בְּמִצְרַיִם וְעֶשֶׂר עַל הַיָּם : (ז) עֲשָׂרָה נִסְיוֹנוֹת
נִסּוּ אֲבוֹתֵינוּ אֶת־הַקָּדוֹשׁ בָּרוּךְ הוּא בַּמִּדְבָּר ' שֶׁנֶּאֱמַר וַיְנַסּוּ

---

ten Sayings. In the first chapter of Genesis, the formula, "And
God said", is repeated nine times; and once, implicitly in the words
which preface the Divine institution of marriage, Genesis 2. 18. In
later times, the Jewish Mystics spoke of creation as a series of ten
emanations (*sefiroth*) from the Infinite (*En Sof*). The *En Sof* and
the emanations, however, were conceived as an absolute Unity,
even as the colours of the flame and the flame itself are latent in the
coal.

2 and **3**. These two mishnas emphasize the patience of God in
His dealings with sinning mankind.

2. *ten generations.* See Genesis, chapter 5.

continued provoking him. Wickedness was rife before the generation
that was destroyed by the Flood, and those evil-doers merited a like fate.
Only the long-suffering mercy of God, by waiting for their repentance,
saved them from their deserved doom.

3. *from Noah to Abraham.* Enumerated in Genesis 11. 10f. Noah
is excluded from the number, for he is the tenth in the earlier series.

received the reward. Which the intermediate generations forfeited by
their sinfulness.

4. The strength of Abraham's Faith, and his steadfastness during
many trials.

with ten Sayings, as well as the goodly reward that will be bestowed upon the just who preserve the world that was created with ten Sayings.

2. There were ten generations from Adam to Noah, to make known the patience of God, seeing that all those generations continued provoking him, until he brought upon them the waters of the Flood.

3. There were ten generations from Noah to Abraham, to make known the patience of God, seeing that all those generations continued provoking him, until Abraham our father came, and received the reward they should all have earned.

4. With ten trials our father Abraham was tried, and he stood firm in them all, to make known how great was the love of our father Abraham.

5. Ten miracles were wrought for our fathers in Egypt, and ten at the Sea.

6. Ten plagues did the Holy One, blessed be he, bring upon the Egyptians in Egypt, and ten at the Sea.

7. With ten trials did our fathers try the Holy One, blessed be he, in the wilderness; as it is said, And they have put me to the proof these ten times, and have not hearkened to my voice.

love. That the Patriarch's obedience of God was the outcome of his love of God is expressly stated in Scripture; cf. "Abraham My friend"; lit. "who loved Me" (Isaiah 41. 8).

5 and **6.** Two other Scriptural examples in the ten-group.

5. *ten miracles . . . for our fathers.* Each plague which afflicted the Egyptians was at the same time a miracle for the Israelites ; *e.g.* when darkness descended upon Egypt, "all the children of Israel had light in their dwellings" (Exodus 10. 23).

6. *ten at the sea.* Deduced from the varying phrases in the Song of Moses, Exodus 15 ; *e.g.* "the horse and his rider hath He thrown into the sea"; and "Pharaoh's chariots and his host hath He cast into the sea". The Passover Haggadah quotes comments of several Rabbis who magnified the number considerably.

As in the mishna preceding, commentators endeavour to find in the Biblical text ten instances of miracles and plagues.

7. *trials . . . try.* Such as the murmuring, in Exodus 14. 11, the making of the Golden Calf, and the report of the Spies. "There is a

אֹתִי זֶה עֶשֶׂר פְּעָמִים וְלֹא שָׁמְעוּ בְּקוֹלִי : (ח) עֲשָׂרָה

נִסִּים נַעֲשׂוּ לַאֲבוֹתֵינוּ בְּבֵית הַמִּקְדָּשׁ · לֹא הִפִּילָה אִשָּׁה

מֵרֵיחַ בְּשַׂר הַקֹּדֶשׁ · וְלֹא הִסְרִיחַ בְּשַׂר הַקֹּדֶשׁ מֵעוֹלָם ·

וְלֹא נִרְאָה זְבוּב בְּבֵית הַמַּטְבָּחַיִם · וְלֹא אֵרַע קֶרִי לְכֹהֵן

גָּדוֹל בְּיוֹם הַכִּפֻּרִים · וְלֹא כִבּוּ הַגְּשָׁמִים אֵשׁ שֶׁל-עֲצֵי

הַמַּעֲרָכָה · וְלֹא נִצְּחָה הָרוּחַ אֶת-עַמּוּד הֶעָשָׁן · וְלֹא נִמְצָא

פְּסוּל בָּעֹמֶר וּבִשְׁתֵּי הַלֶּחֶם וּבְלֶחֶם הַפָּנִים · עוֹמְדִים צְפוּפִים

וּמִשְׁתַּחֲוִים רְוָחִים · וְלֹא הִזִּיק נָחָשׁ וְעַקְרָב בִּירוּשָׁלַיִם

מֵעוֹלָם · וְלֹא אָמַר אָדָם לַחֲבֵרוֹ צַר לִי הַמָּקוֹם שֶׁאָלִין

בִּירוּשָׁלָיִם : (ט) עֲשָׂרָה דְבָרִים נִבְרְאוּ בְּעֶרֶב שַׁבָּת בֵּין

certain daring simplicity, which perhaps only a Jew can fully appreciate, in this linking together of the trials which God and Israel brought on each other " (Herford).

8. Ten Wonders associated with the Temple in Rabbinic literature. It is an attempt to magnify the holiness of the Temple in terms of miracle. These wonders are not in the Bible, but are due to the pious love of both people and priest for the Central Sanctuary, and especially after its destruction by the Romans.

the holy flesh. Of the sacrifices. The flesh could only be eaten by the priests ; but no harmful effect occurred to any one in whom the odour created a longing to partake of it.

never became putrid. Although it often remained in a heated atmosphere for several days.

no unclean accident. Which would have rendered him unfit to officiate on that Sacred Day in the Sanctuary.

wood-pile. The altar was in an uncovered court, open to the sky.

column of smoke. In ordinary circumstances the wind would at times have blown the smoke downwards, and inconvenienced the priests.

the omer. See Leviticus 23. 19f. The sheaf of barley was cut on the second night of Passover for the wave-offering, and prepared for presentation the following day. If any defect had been discovered in the flour, there would not have been time to provide another supply.

the two loaves. See Leviticus 23. 17. They had to be baked before the commencement of the Festival, and no substitute could be found if at the last moment they were disqualified by a defect.

8. Ten miracles were wrought for our fathers in the Temple : no woman miscarried from the scent of the holy flesh ; the holy flesh never became putrid ; no fly was seen in the slaughter house ; no unclean accident ever befell the high priest on the Day of Atonement ; the rain never quenched the fire of the wood-pile on the altar ; neither did the wind overcome the column of smoke that arose therefrom ; nor was there ever found any disqualifying defect in the omer, or in the two loaves (on Pentecost), or in the shewbread ; though the people stood closely pressed together, they found ample space to prostrate themselves ; never did serpent or scorpion injure anyone in Jerusalem ; nor did any man ever say to his fellow, The place is too narrow for me to lodge over night in Jerusalem.

9. Ten things were created on the eve of Sabbath in the

---

the shewbread. See Leviticus 24. 5f. It was changed each Sabbath, and the fresh supply baked before the Holy Day. The stale bread would have had to remain a second week, contrary to the law if anything was wrong with the new.

closely pressed together. On the Festivals and Day of Atonement the precincts of the Temple were thronged to their utmost capacity.

prostrate themselves. On the Day of Atonement, as the High Priest pronounced the Divine Name in making the confession of sins.

serpent or scorpion. Although they were to be found in the city.

to lodge over night. Even on the Festivals, when every Israelite made a pilgrimage to Jerusalem, there was sufficient accommodation for the multitudes. Josephus gives fabulous figures of those who came to celebrate Passover in the Holy City. These last two miracles which, as the Talmud points out, relate not to the Temple but to Jerusalem, are capable of telling homiletic application, especially in regard to the broad tolerance of Israel's teaching. Thus, neither serpent-bite nor scorpion-sting was prevalent in Jerusalem: there have been no Inquisitions in Judaism. Nor has any man reason to say, "Judaism is too narrow for me to find spiritual lodgment therein ".

9. " All phenomena that seemed to partake at once of the natural and the supernatural, were conceived as having had their origin in the interval between the close of the work of Creation and the commencement of the Sabbath " (Singer). In this way, the Rabbis gave expression to their conception of the miraculous in the scheme of things. Miracles, they held, were not interruptions of Nature's laws : at Creation, God had provided for them in advance, as part of the cosmic plan. " The Fathers of the Mishna, who taught that Balaam's ass was created in

הַשְּׁמָשׁוֹת וְאֵלּוּ הֵן · פִּי הָאָרֶץ פִּי הַבְּאֵר פִּי הָאָתוֹן
הַקֶּשֶׁת וְהַמָּן וְהַמַּטֶּה וְהַשָּׁמִיר הַכְּתָב וְהַמִּכְתָּב וְהַלֻּחוֹת ·
וְיֵשׁ אוֹמְרִים אַף הַמַּזִּיקִין וּקְבוּרָתוֹ שֶׁל־מֹשֶׁה וְאֵילוֹ שֶׁל־
אַבְרָהָם אָבִינוּ · וְיֵשׁ אוֹמְרִים אַף צְבָת בִּצְבָת עֲשׂוּיָה :

the eve of the Sabbath, in the twilight, were not fantastic fools, but
subtle philosophers, discovering the reign of universal law through the
exceptions, the miracles that had to be created specially and were
still a part of the order of the world, bound to appear in due time much
as apparently erratic comets are '' (Zangwill).

eve of the Sabbath. At the end of the sixth day of Creation.

mouth of the earth. Which engulfed Korah and his associates;
Numbers 16. 32.

mouth of the well. Tradition relates that this well, named after
Miriam, accompanied the Iṡraelites in the journey through the wilderness; Numbers 21. 16.

mouth of the ass. Which spoke to Balaam; Numbers 22. 28. See
'' Balaam and the Ass '', *Numbers,* 237 (Soncino, 671).

the rainbow. See Genesis 9. 13f. According to the Rabbis, the
rainbow existed since the very dawn of Creation. The rainbow—that
everlasting symbol of Hope—was thus created contemporaneously
with the appearance of man. Hope springs eternal in the human
breast, and is an essential part of human nature. Man enters the world
with hope ; he bears up against all toils and sorrows through hope ;
and when his days on earth are nearing their end, he plants Hope on
the grave. Every item in this wonderful mishna is a spiritual hiero-
glyph ; see '' Man's Spiritual Equipment '' in Hertz, *Sermons* I, 170f.

the manna. See Exodus 16. 14f.

the rod. Wherewith Moses performed God's signs in Egypt;
Exodus 4. 17. According to legend, it belonged to Adam, and was
handed down through the generations to Moses.

the Shamir. The Altar had to be built of rough and unhewn stones ;
no sword or iron—symbols of violence and discord—could be lifted up
in connection with the Altar which stood for peace, unity, and recon-
ciliation. As no hammer or axe was used, how were the stones fitted
together ? the people asked. And Jewish folk-belief answered by telling
that Solomon in his wisdom came into possession of a wonderful worm,
one of the marvels of creation, the Shamir, which when placed upon
even the hardest stones would instantly cleave them as desired, and all
as easily and noiselessly as the leaves of a book open. Many were the
miraculous deeds—legend tells—that were performed by its help, till,
with the destruction of the Temple, the Shamir disappeared from earth.

the writing on the tables. Of the Decalogue delivered by God
to Moses, which are described as '' written on both their sides ''

twilight : the mouth of the earth ; the mouth of the well ; the mouth of the ass ; the rainbow ; the manna ; the rod of Moses ; the Shamir ; the writing on the tables ; the instrument of writing, and the tables of stone : some say, the destroying spirits also, and the sepulchre of Moses, and the ram of Abraham our father ; and others say, tongs also made with tongs.

(Exodus 82. 15). Traditionally, the letters were cut through the stone, so that the words were legible on both sides ; and letters thus cut would have fallen out but were held in place in a miraculous manner.

instrument of writing. Engraving tool.

tables of stone. " The tables were the work of God " (Exodus 82. 16) *i.e.* miraculously made. This was one way of teaching the pre-existence and eternal validity of the Decalogue.

destroying spirits. Demons figure in Rabbinic folk-lore, and belief in their reality was widespread; but, as here, they are held to be absolutely the *creatures* of God; see p. 264. Later Jewish teachers —the Gaon Samuel ibn Chofni (died 1034), and Abraham ibn Ezra (1104–1167)—are among the first in the history of the world to deny the exist-ence of demons. Not the least meaning-laden among the things here enumerated, is the thought that " demons ", *e.g.* the forces of tempta-tion and unrest in man, date from the dawn of Creation, and are part of the equipment of the human soul from its birth. It is true that, when these forces dominate us, they are " destroying spirits ". But when these instincts are properly controlled, when we rule *them*, they are the driving-forces in life. It is the capacity to fight evil, or to succumb to evil, that distinguishes man from the brute. And it is because of evil and suffering and temptation, that life is the glorious battlefield it is. We are at once the combatants and the combat and the field that is torn with strife. But in this struggle we are not left groping in the dark. Simultaneously with the destroying passions of man, the " Tables of the Law " together with " the Writing on the Tables " were created. As those instincts towards evil are part of the original constitution of man, so also are conscience and the holy laws of right and wrong, that are to control those instincts.

sepulchre of Moses. Deuteronomy 84. 6. As no man knows its loca-tion, it must have been made by God. Its pre-existence teaches, "Moses died : who shall not die ? "

ram of Abraham. Genesis 22. 13. It was pre-ordained that the ram, in connection with the sacrifice of Isaac, be at hand in the thicket at that time. In this way, the whole idea of sacrifice and martyrdom was conceived as part of the Divine Plan. On the ideal of martyrdom in Judaism, see p. 256.

tongs also made with tongs. This mishna attempts to solve the prob-lem, Who made the tongs which held the first tongs whilst they were being made ?

(י) שִׁבְעָה דְבָרִים בְּגֹלֶם וְשִׁבְעָה בְחָכָם · חָכָם אֵינוֹ
מְדַבֵּר לִפְנֵי מִי שֶׁגָּדוֹל מִמֶּנּוּ בְּחָכְמָה · וְאֵינוֹ נִכְנָס
לְתוֹךְ דִּבְרֵי חֲבֵרוֹ · וְאֵינוֹ נִבְהָל לְהָשִׁיב · שׁוֹאֵל כָּעִנְיָן
וּמֵשִׁיב כַּהֲלָכָה · וְאוֹמֵר עַל־רִאשׁוֹן רִאשׁוֹן וְעַל־אַחֲרוֹן
אַחֲרוֹן · וְעַל מַה־שֶּׁלֹא שָׁמַע אוֹמֵר לֹא שָׁמַעְתִּי · וּמוֹדֶה
עַל־הָאֱמֶת · וְחִלּוּפֵיהֶם בְּגֹלֶם : (יא) שִׁבְעָה מִינֵי פֻּרְעָנִיּוֹת
בָּאִים לָעוֹלָם עַל־שִׁבְעָה גּוּפֵי עֲבֵרָה : מִקְצָתָם מְעַשְּׂרִים
וּמִקְצָתָם אֵינָם מְעַשְּׂרִים רָעָב שֶׁל־בַּצֹּרֶת בָּא מִקְצָתָם רְעֵבִים
וּמִקְצָתָם שְׂבֵעִים · גָּמְרוּ שֶׁלֹא לְעַשֵּׂר רָעָב שֶׁל־מְהוּמָה וְשֶׁל־
בַּצֹּרֶת בָּא · וְשֶׁלֹא לִטּוֹל אֶת־הַחַלָּה רָעָב שֶׁל־כְּלָיָה בָּא ·
דֶּבֶר בָּא לָעוֹלָם עַל־מִיתוֹת הָאֲמוּרוֹת בַּתּוֹרָה שֶׁלֹא נִמְסְרוּ

10–11. Two seven-groups of Sayings.

10. Enumerates the distinguishing marks of the " wise man " in his conversation, this being the mirror of a man's inner refinement.

uncultured. Heb. *golem* ; lit. " the embryo ". Here the word is used of a man with an undeveloped mentality. In later legends, *golem* means a clay or wooden figure endowed with life by mystic use of the Divine Name.

wise man. Heb. *chochom*, the man reared in the Torah.

does not break in. He waits until the other has finished what he had to say, before commenting upon his statement.

not hasty to answer. He deliberates, before raising an objection to a statement.

according to the subject matter. Relevant to the theme under discussion.

first thing first. His mind works in orderly sequence.

not understood. Or, " not heard " ; *i.e.* if he has no tradition regarding a matter, he states it.

he acknowledges the truth. One of the crowning signs of true culture : if another's argument is more cogent than his own, or if he has been shown his error, he readily admits it.

11. Seven Forms of Retribution for seven Chief Transgressions.

It is not a philosophy of suffering, but a rough-and-ready way of accounting for evils by the principle of "measure for measure". The transgressions are ritual, ethical, juristic, and social ; and thus cover the whole sphere of the religious life.

V

10, 11

Sayings of the Fathers

10. There are seven marks of an uncultured, and seven of a wise man. The wise man does not speak before him who is greater than he in wisdom ; and does not break in upon the speech of his fellow ; he is not hasty to answer ; he questions according to the subject matter, and answers to the point ; he speaks upon the first thing first, and the last last ; regarding that which he has not understood he says, I do not understand it ; and he acknowledges the truth. The reverse of all this is to be found in an uncultured man.

11. Seven kinds of punishment come into the world for seven important transgressions. ¹If some give their tithes and others do not, a dearth ensues from drought, and some suffer hunger while others are full. ²If they all determine to give no tithes, a dearth ensues from tumult and drought. ³If they resolve not to give the dough-cake, an exterminating dearth ensues. ⁴Pestilence comes into the world to fulfil those death penalties threatened in the Torah, the execution of which, however, is not within the function of a human tribunal ; and for the violation of the law regarding the

---

the world. Here it means, as in 1, 2, the Jewish People.
important transgressions. Or, " categories of transgression ".

(*a*), (*b*) and (*c*) Dearth : for Withholding of tithes to priest and poor.
dearth ensues from drought. The punishment corresponds to the offence. Those who cause priest, widow and the poor to hunger will themselves suffer hunger.
tumult. Of war, which will prevent them from gathering the harvest.
resolve not to give. *i.e.* in addition to withholding the tithe.
dough-cake. Heb. חלה ; if even the women refuse to do their duty in holy things, the drought will be complete. Cf. Leviticus 26. 9. It was the special obligation of woman to carry out the precept in Numbers 15. 20. For its observance at the present day, see *Numbers*, 153 (Soncino, 632).

(*d*) Pestilence : for Failure to punish crime and Callousness towards the poor.
death penalties. They were crimes to be punished by " death at the hands of Heaven ", and were to be expiated by means of such pestilence. Or, the guilty were not discovered and, if discovered, could not be punished for technical reasons.

לְבֵית דִין וְעַל פֵּרוֹת שְׁבִיעִית · חֶרֶב בָּאָה לָעוֹלָם עַל־עִנּוּי

הַדִּין וְעַל־עִוּוּת הַדִּין וְעַל־הַמּוֹרִים בַּתּוֹרָה שֶׁלֹּא כַהֲלָכָה ·

חַיָּה רָעָה בָּאָה לָעוֹלָם עַל־שְׁבוּעַת שָׁוְא וְעַל־חִלּוּל הַשֵּׁם ·

גָּלוּת בָּאָה לָעוֹלָם עַל־עֲבוֹדַת אֱלִילִים וְעַל־גִּלּוּי עֲרָיוֹת וְעַל־

שְׁפִיכוּת דָּמִים וְעַל־שְׁמִטַּת הָאָרֶץ : (יב) בְּאַרְבָּעָה פְרָקִים

הַדֶּבֶר מִתְרַבֶּה · בָּרְבִיעִית וּבַשְּׁבִיעִית וּבְמוֹצָאֵי שְׁבִיעִית

וּבְמוֹצָאֵי הֶחָג שֶׁבְּכָל־שָׁנָה וְשָׁנָה : בָּרְבִיעִית מִפְּנֵי מַעְשַׂר

עָנִי שֶׁבַּשְּׁלִישִׁית · בַּשְּׁבִיעִית מִפְּנֵי מַעְשַׂר עָנִי שֶׁבַּשִּׁשִּׁית ·

בְּמוֹצָאֵי שְׁבִיעִית מִפְּנֵי פֵּרוֹת שְׁבִיעִית · בְּמוֹצָאֵי הֶחָג

seventh year. Commanded to be observed as a Sabbath-year of the field (Leviticus 25. 1–7). No agricultural work was to be undertaken. What the soil produced had to be eaten by the owner's household, or by the poor, but it was not to be bartered ; *Leviticus,* 266 (Soncino, 531). Callousness towards the poor is deemed as grievous a moral calamity as failure to punish capital offenders; see next mishna.

(*e*) The Sword : for Delay and Perversion of Justice.

delay of justice. More than the proverbial " law's delay " ; *undue* postponement of a judicial decision.

perversion of justice. Condemning the innocent, and freeing the guilty—an infamy denounced by the Prophets as the cardinal sin in any human society.

interpret the Torah . . . sense. Forbidding what is permitted, and permitting what is forbidden.

If justice is the foundation of a nation and of its friendly relations with other nations, then the breakdown of the machinery of justice or its perversion, necessarily leads sooner or later to armed conflict with other peoples. Since the days of Amos, it was the repeated warning of Prophecy that the sword is the Divine punishment for injustice (Beer).

(*f*) Wild Beasts : for Perjury and Chillul Hashem.

The nation's disintegration becomes greater, as the crimes become more unpardonable. In time of warfare, when the land is desolated, wild beasts multiply. Throughout the Biblical period, the country was at no time so settled that the jungle lay beyond the range of ordinary experience ; so much so, that the promise of the wild beasts being tamed was one of the elements in the Messianic age. Wild beasts must have increased after the devastations of the land under Titus and Hadrian.

fruits of the seventh year. ⁵The sword comes into the world for the delay of justice, and for the perversion of justice, and on account of the offence of those who interpret the Torah not according to its true sense. ⁶Wild beasts come into the world for perjury, and for the profanation of the Divine Name. ⁷Captivity comes into the world on account of idolatry, immorality, bloodshed, and the neglect of the year of rest for the soil.

12. At four periods pestilence grows apace : in the fourth year, in the seventh, at the conclusion of the seventh year, and at the conclusion of the Feast of Tabernacles in each year : in the fourth year, for default of giving the tithe to the poor in the third year ; in the seventh year, for default of giving the tithe to the poor in the sixth year ; at the conclusion of the seventh year, for the violation of the law regarding the fruits of the seventh year, and at the conclusion of the Feast of Tabernacles in each year, for robbing the poor of the grants legally assigned to them.

profanation of the Name. Homiletically, this saying contains a grave warning : Wherever Jews treat the Oath of Sinai as a vain oath ; that is, wherever Jews are guilty of conduct unworthy of their Faith, there the wild beast in man—blind prejudice and causeless hatred—is unchained against Israel.

(*g*) Exile and captivity : For Idolatry, Immorality and Bloodshed.

These crimes bring with them the crowning catastrophe. The total uprooting of the nation by transportation to a distant foreign land. Each of these three sins the Jew is forbidden to commit, even if threatened with death for his refusal.
year of rest for the soil. The Sabbatical year when the earth lies fallow ; see Leviticus 25. 3f.

12–18. Seven four-groups of Sayings.
12. *pestilence.* This paragraph amplifies what had been stated in the preceding mishna : " Pestilence comes into the world . . . for the violation of the law regarding the fruits of the seventh year ".
robbing the poor. The Torah prescribed that the poor were to receive the gleanings, the corners of the field, and forgotten sheaves (Leviticus 19. 9, Deuteronomy 24. 19). The Feast of Tabernacles was harvesting time. It was then that most of these offences were committed ; therefore, punishment was experienced at that period of the year.

שֶׁבְּכָל־שָׁנָה וְשָׁנָה מִפְּנֵי גֶזֶל מַתְּנוֹת עֲנִיִּים : (יג) אַרְבַּע
מִדּוֹת בְּאָדָם · הָאוֹמֵר שֶׁלִּי שֶׁלִּי וְשֶׁלְּךָ שֶׁלָּךְ זוֹ מִדָּה
בֵּינוֹנִית וְיֵשׁ אוֹמְרִים זוֹ מִדַּת סְדוֹם · שֶׁלִּי שֶׁלָּךְ וְשֶׁלְּךָ
שֶׁלִּי עַם הָאָרֶץ · שֶׁלִּי שֶׁלָּךְ וְשֶׁלְּךָ שֶׁלָּךְ חָסִיד · שֶׁלָּךְ
שֶׁלִּי וְשֶׁלִּי שֶׁלִּי רָשָׁע : (יד) אַרְבַּע מִדּוֹת בְּדֵעוֹת · נוֹחַ
לִכְעוֹס וְנוֹחַ לִרְצוֹת יָצָא הֶפְסֵדוֹ בִּשְׂכָרוֹ · קָשֶׁה לִכְעוֹס
וְקָשֶׁה לִרְצוֹת יָצָא שְׂכָרוֹ בְּהֶפְסֵדוֹ · קָשֶׁה לִכְעוֹס וְנוֹחַ
לִרְצוֹת חָסִיד · נוֹחַ לִכְעוֹס וְקָשֶׁה לִרְצוֹת רָשָׁע : (טו) אַרְבַּע
מִדּוֹת בְּתַלְמִידִים · מָהִיר לִשְׁמוֹעַ וּמָהִיר לְאַבֵּד יָצָא שְׂכָרוֹ
בְּהֶפְסֵדוֹ · קָשֶׁה לִשְׁמוֹעַ וְקָשֶׁה לְאַבֵּד יָצָא הֶפְסֵדוֹ בִּשְׂכָרוֹ ·
מָהִיר לִשְׁמוֹעַ וְקָשֶׁה לְאַבֵּד זוֹ חֵלֶק טוֹב · קָשֶׁה לִשְׁמוֹעַ
וּמָהִיר לְאַבֵּד זוֹ חֵלֶק רָע : (טז) אַרְבַּע מִדּוֹת בְּנוֹתְנֵי
צְדָקָה. הָרוֹצֶה שֶׁיִּתֵּן וְלֹא יִתְּנוּ אֲחֵרִים עֵינוֹ רָעָה בְּשֶׁל־
אֲחֵרִים · יִתְּנוּ אֲחֵרִים וְהוּא לֹא יִתֵּן עֵינוֹ רָעָה בְּשֶׁלּוֹ · יִתֵּן

The connection between transgression and such scourges as famine
and pestilence was a settled belief of the Talmudic teachers. Moderns
may scoff at this belief; yet it is a sound instinct which in all ages has felt
that retribution must follow, in some form, upon all transgression. "In
the economy of the universe there may be ends of a purely physical
kind served by such disasters, apart altogether from their meaning to
man. But man at least learns from them that nature does not exist
solely for feeding, clothing, and keeping him wealthy" (G. A. Smith).

13. Four types of Men.

neutral character. Some consider such an attitude to be unethical.
It resembles that of Sodom, whose motto seems to have been, "each
man for himself"; cf. Ezekiel, 16. 49, "Behold this was the iniquity
of thy sister Sodom . . . neither did she strengthen the hand of the
poor and the needy". What a man has is not entirely his own. He
should recognize the claims of charity.

boor. Heb. *am ha-aretz*; see on II, 6. Social stability is impossible
upon his theory.

V

13-16

*Sayings
of the
Fathers*

13. There are four characters among men : he who says, What is mine is mine and what is thine is thine, his is a neutral character (some say, this is a character like that of Sodom) ; he who says, What is mine is thine and what is thine is mine, is a boor ; he who says, What is mine is thine and what is thine is thine, is a saint ; he who says, What is thine is mine and what is mine is mine, is a wicked man.

14. There are four kinds of tempers : he whom it is easy to provoke and easy to pacify, his loss disappears in his gain ; he whom it is hard to provoke and hard to pacify, his gain disappears in his loss ; he whom it is hard to provoke and easy to pacify is a saint ; he whom it is easy to provoke and hard to pacify is a wicked man.

15. There are four qualities in disciples : he who quickly understands and quickly forgets, his gain disappears in his loss ; he who understands with difficulty and forgets with difficulty, his loss disappears in his gain ; he who understands quickly and forgets with difficulty, his is a good portion ; he who understands with difficulty and forgets quickly, his is an evil portion.

16. As to almsgiving there are four dispositions : he who desires to give, but that others should not give, his eye is evil towards what appertains to others ; he who desires that others should give, but will not give himself, his eye is

---

saint. He asks nothing of others, and is ready to give what he has to help the poor.

wicked man. His temperament is that of a robber.

14. Four different dispositions.

saint. It should be noted that he is " hard ", not *impossible,* " to provoke ". Even the best men occasionally give way to anger ; and always to *indignation* at an outrage against decency and right.

15. Four types of students. As no ethical principle is involved, the terms " saint " and " wicked " are not used in this estimate of the intellectual qualities of the student.

16. Four kinds of almsgivers.

his eye is evil. Cf. II, 14. He does not like to see others gain merit and blessing by their charitable acts.

ה
פרקי
אבות

וְיִתֵּן אֲחֵרִים חָסִיד · לֹא יִתֵּן וְלֹא יִתְּנוּ אֲחֵרִים רָשָׁע :
(יז) אַרְבַּע מִדּוֹת בְּהוֹלְכֵי בֵית הַמִּדְרָשׁ · הוֹלֵךְ וְאֵינוֹ עֹשֶׂה
שְׂכַר הֲלִיכָה בְּיָדוֹ · עֹשֶׂה וְאֵינוֹ הוֹלֵךְ שְׂכַר מַעֲשֶׂה בְּיָדוֹ ·
הוֹלֵךְ וְעֹשֶׂה חָסִיד · לֹא הוֹלֵךְ וְלֹא עֹשֶׂה רָשָׁע : (יח) אַרְבַּע
מִדּוֹת בְּיוֹשְׁבִים לִפְנֵי חֲכָמִים · סְפוֹג וּמַשְׁפֵּךְ מְשַׁמֶּרֶת וְנָפָה ·
סְפוֹג שֶׁהוּא סוֹפֵג אֶת־הַכֹּל · וּמַשְׁפֵּךְ שֶׁמַּכְנִיס בְּזוֹ וּמוֹצִיא
בְזוֹ · מְשַׁמֶּרֶת שֶׁמּוֹצִיאָה אֶת־הַיַּיִן וְקוֹלֶטֶת אֶת־הַשְּׁמָרִים ·
וְנָפָה שֶׁמּוֹצִיאָה אֶת־הַקֶּמַח וְקוֹלֶטֶת אֶת־הַסֹּלֶת : (יט) כָּל־
אַהֲבָה שֶׁהִיא־תְלוּיָה בְדָבָר בָּטֵל דָּבָר בְּטֵלָה אַהֲבָה ·
וְשֶׁאֵינָהּ תְּלוּיָה בְדָבָר אֵינָהּ בְּטֵלָה לְעוֹלָם · אֵיזוֹ הִיא
אַהֲבָה שֶׁהִיא־תְלוּיָה בְדָבָר זוֹ אַהֲבַת אַמְנוֹן וְתָמָר · וְשֶׁאֵינָהּ
תְּלוּיָה בְדָבָר זוֹ אַהֲבַת דָּוִד וִיהוֹנָתָן : (כ) כָּל־מַחֲלֹקֶת

against what is his own. He begrudges himself the acquisition of merit.

a saint. He evinces the right ethical spirit.

a wicked man. He has no sympathy for the needy in their distress.

17. Four classes of those who attend in the Beth Hamidrash, to learn their religious duty or some spiritual lesson.

does not practise. The moral lessons which he heard expounded.

reward for going. His attendance was at least proof of a desire to learn, and he received his reward for that.

he who practises. By copying the example of the pious man, but without obtaining his inspiration from hearing the exposition of the Torah.

18. Four kinds of disciples, and their capacity to distinguish between good doctrine and bad, between what is of primary and secondary importance. The distinction applies also to schoolchildren of all times.

sucks up everything. Absorbs the true and the false, the sublime and the trivial.

lets in at one end and out at the other. Typifies the student or child that forgets everything, though he learns readily.

retains the lees. He remembers only the worst of whatever he hears or reads.

V

evil against what is his own ; he who gives and wishes others to give, is a saint ; he who will not give and does not wish others to give, is a wicked man.

17. There are four characters suggested by those who attend the house of study : he who goes and does not practise, secures the reward for going ; he who practises but does not go, secures the reward for practising ; he who goes and practises, is a saint ; he who neither goes nor practises, is a wicked man.

18. There are four qualities among those that sit before the wise : they are like a sponge, a funnel, a strainer, or a sieve : a sponge, which sucks up everything ; a funnel, which lets in at one end and out at the other ; a strainer, which lets the wine pass out and retains the lees ; a sieve, which lets out the bran and retains the fine flour.

19. Whenever love depends upon some material cause, with the passing away of that cause, the love too passes away ; but if it be not dependent upon such a cause, it will not pass away for ever. Which love was that which depended upon a material cause ? Such was the love of Amnon and Tamar. And that which depended upon no such cause ? Such was the love of David and Jonathan.

---

lets out the bran. He lets go the worthless and retains the good. Like Rabbi Meir, who stated of his relations to Acher (see IV, 25) that he ate the fruit of his learning—its Jewish content—and threw away the husk. The sieve spoken of, is one which retains the fine flour in a receptacle attached to the machine, and is so constructed that the coarse grain passes out at the end of the sieve (Taylor).

19–22. General Moral Reflections.
19. Two kinds of love.
material cause. Such love only seeks gratification of self, and passes away with the attainment of that gratification.
Amnon and Tamar. See II Samuel 13.
David and Jonathan. The most sublime story of disinterested friendship, based on unselfish mutual affection. " The soul of Jonathan was knit with the soul of David, and Jonathan loved him as his own soul " (I Samuel 18. 1), although he knew that David stood between him and the throne.

שֶׁהִיא לְשֵׁם שָׁמַיִם סוֹפָהּ לְהִתְקַיֵּם וְשֶׁאֵינָהּ לְשֵׁם שָׁמַיִם

אֵין סוֹפָהּ לְהִתְקַיֵּם ׳ אֵיזוֹ הִיא מַחֲלֹקֶת שֶׁהִיא לְשֵׁם שָׁמַיִם

זוֹ מַחֲלֹקֶת הִלֵּל וְשַׁמַּי ׳ וְשֶׁאֵינָהּ לְשֵׁם שָׁמַיִם זוֹ מַחֲלֹקֶת

קֹרַח וְכָל־עֲדָתוֹ : (כא) כָּל־הַמְזַכֶּה אֶת־הָרַבִּים אֵין חֵטְא

בָּא עַל־יָדוֹ וְכָל־הַמַּחֲטִיא אֶת־הָרַבִּים אֵין־מַסְפִּיקִים בְּיָדוֹ

לַעֲשׂוֹת תְּשׁוּבָה ׳ מֹשֶׁה זָכָה וְזִכָּה אֶת־הָרַבִּים זְכוּת הָרַבִּים

תָּלוּי בּוֹ ׳ שֶׁנֶּאֱמַר צִדְקַת יְיָ עָשָׂה וּמִשְׁפָּטָיו עִם־יִשְׂרָאֵל ׳ יָרָבְעָם

בֶּן־נְבָט חָטָא וְהֶחֱטִיא אֶת־הָרַבִּים חֵטְא הָרַבִּים תָּלוּי בּוֹ ׳

שֶׁנֶּאֱמַר עַל־חַטֹּאות יָרָבְעָם אֲשֶׁר חָטָא וַאֲשֶׁר הֶחֱטִיא אֶת־

יִשְׂרָאֵל : (כב) כָּל־מִי שֶׁיֵּשׁ־בּוֹ שְׁלֹשָׁה דְבָרִים הַלָּלוּ הוּא

מִתַּלְמִידָיו שֶׁל־אַבְרָהָם אָבִינוּ ׳ וּשְׁלֹשָׁה דְבָרִים אֲחֵרִים הוּא

מִתַּלְמִידָיו שֶׁל־בִּלְעָם הָרָשָׁע ׳ עַיִן טוֹבָה וְרוּחַ נְמוּכָה וְנֶפֶשׁ

20. On religious controversy : honest and dishonest.

controversy that is in the name of Heaven. Cf. IV, 14. The discussion is conducted with a sincere desire to reach the truth.

Hillel and Shammai. They and their Schools differed on many points that were keenly debated between them. Since their aim was nothing else than the correct exposition of the Torah, the Talmud related that a *Bath-kol* (see VI, 2) proclaimed, "They both speak the words of the living God".

Korah and his company. Numbers 16. Their controversy with Moses and Aaron was merely a rebellion against authority, and due to their ambition to supplant these leaders. It met with a tragic end.

21. On moral leaders and misleaders.

to be righteous. To lead lives dominated by Religion, Worship and Beneficence.

no sin shall be brought about. The righteousness of the many that they have learned from him, acts as a defence to him, and he does not become the cause of sin.

shall not have the means to repent. It would be unjust if he escaped punishment by means of penitence, while those whom he had misled suffered. The sins he led others to commit rise in judgment against him, and these sins are beyond the remedial action of his own repentance; see Yoma 87a. "There is a fine chivalry in this Jewish doctrine. [98]

V
20-22

*Sayings
of the
Fathers*

20. Every controversy that is in the name of Heaven, shall in the end lead to a permanent result; but every controversy that is not in the name of Heaven, shall not lead to a permanent result. Which controversy was that which was in the name of Heaven ? Such was the controversy of Hillel and Shammai. And that which was not in the name of Heaven ? Such was the controversy of Korah and all his company.

21. Whosoever causes many to be righteous, through him no sin shall be brought about ; but he who causes many to sin, shall not have the means to repent. Moses was righteous and made many righteous ; the righteousness 21 of the many was laid upon him, as it is said, He executed the justice of the Lord, and his judgments with Israel. Jeroboam, the son of Nebat, sinned and caused many to sin ; the sin of the many was laid upon him, as it is said, For the sins of Jeroboam which he sinned, and wherewith he made Israel to sin.

22. Whosoever has these three attributes, is of the disciples of Abraham our father; but whosoever has three other attributes, is of the disciples of Balaam the wicked. A good eye, a humble mind and a lowly spirit (are the tokens) of the disciples of Abraham our father ; an evil eye,

Jewish teachers alone have had the moral insight to discern, and the wisdom to teach, this lesson " (Herford).

causes many to sin. The climax in the Confession on the Atonement Day is, *we have led astray.*

22. *disciples of Abraham . . . . Balaam.* By the time this mishna was composed, the figure of Balaam had come to typify low heathen viciousness of thought and action; see *Numbers*, 228 (Soncino, 668). Note that the contrast is not between Abraham and Balaam, but between their *disciples :* a religious system is judged not by its founders, but by the lives that their followers after them lead. The purpose of this mishna seems to stress the fact that selfishness, pride and haughtiness are un-Jewish vices. The characterization of the followers of Balaam is harsh, but—as a Christian commentator admits— so were the attacks on Jews by contemporaries of the author of this saying.

שְׁפָלָה מִתַּלְמִידָיו שֶׁל־אַבְרָהָם אָבִינוּ ׃ עַיִן רָעָה וְרוּחַ גְּבוֹהָה

וְנֶפֶשׁ רְחָבָה מִתַּלְמִידָיו שֶׁל־בִּלְעָם הָרָשָׁע ׃ מַה בֵּין תַּלְמִידָיו

שֶׁל־אַבְרָהָם אָבִינוּ לְתַלְמִידָיו שֶׁל־בִּלְעָם הָרָשָׁע ׃ תַּלְמִידָיו

שֶׁל־אַבְרָהָם אָבִינוּ אוֹכְלִים בָּעוֹלָם הַזֶּה וְנוֹחֲלִים הָעוֹלָם

הַבָּא ׃ שֶׁנֶּאֱמַר לְהַנְחִיל אֹהֲבַי יֵשׁ וְאֹצְרֹתֵיהֶם אֲמַלֵּא ׃

תַּלְמִידָיו שֶׁל־בִּלְעָם הָרָשָׁע יוֹרְשִׁים גֵּי־הִנֹּם וְיוֹרְדִים לִבְאֵר

שַׁחַת ׃ שֶׁנֶּאֱמַר וְאַתָּה אֱלֹהִים תּוֹרִדֵם לִבְאֵר שַׁחַת אַנְשֵׁי

דָמִים וּמִרְמָה לֹא־יֶחֱצוּ יְמֵיהֶם וַאֲנִי אֶבְטַח־בָּךְ ׃ (כג) יְהוּדָה

בֶּן־תֵּימָא אוֹמֵר ׃ הֱוֵי עַז כַּנָּמֵר וְקַל כַּנֶּשֶׁר רָץ כַּצְּבִי וְגִבּוֹר

כָּאֲרִי לַעֲשׂוֹת רְצוֹן אָבִיךָ שֶׁבַּשָּׁמָיִם ׃ הוּא הָיָה אוֹמֵר ׃

עַז פָּנִים לְגֵי־הִנֹּם וּבוֹשׁ פָּנִים לְגַן עֵדֶן ׃ יְהִי רָצוֹן מִלְפָנֶיךָ

יְיָ אֱלֹהֵינוּ וֵאלֹהֵי אֲבוֹתֵינוּ שֶׁיִּבָּנֶה בֵּית הַמִּקְדָּשׁ בִּמְהֵרָה

בְיָמֵינוּ וְתֵן חֶלְקֵנוּ בְּתוֹרָתֶךָ ׃ (כד) הוּא הָיָה אֹמֵר ׃ בֶּן־

חָמֵשׁ שָׁנִים לַמִּקְרָא בֶּן־עֶשֶׂר שָׁנִים לַמִּשְׁנָה בֶּן־שְׁלֹשׁ עֶשְׂרֵה

---

proud spirit. An ambitious nature.

what is the difference ? In the fate which is in store for them.

that love me. Said of Abraham in the Hebrew of Isaiah 41. 8.

substance. In a spiritual sense of the Hereafter.

treasuries. The boon of this world.

Gehinnom. See on I, 5.

blood-thirsty and deceitful men. According to tradition, it was Balaam's sinister counsel that was responsible for the death of 24,000 (Numbers 25. 9).

23-26. CLOSE OF THE TRACTATE.

23. *Judah, the son of Tema.* It is unknown in which century he lived, or who his teacher was.

bold as a leopard. As this animal is fearless and cannot be turned aside from stalking its prey, so the Israelite should permit nothing to stand in the way of the carrying out of his Jewish and human duties.

light as an eagle. This phrase and " strong as a lion " are taken from II Samuel 1. 28.

V

23, 24

Sayings of the Fathers

a haughty mind and a proud spirit (are the signs) of the disciples of Balaam the wicked. What is the difference between the disciples of Abraham our father and those of Balaam the wicked ? The disciples of Abraham our father enjoy this world and inherit the world to come ; as it is said, That I may cause those that love me to inherit substance, and may fill all their treasuries. The disciples of Balaam the wicked inherit Gehinnom and descend into the pit of destruction ; as it is said, But thou, O God, wilt bring them down into the pit of destruction : blood-thirsty and deceitful men shall not live out half their days ; but I will trust in thee.

23. Judah, the son of Tema, said, Be strong as a leopard, light as an eagle, fleet as a hart, and strong as a lion, to do the will of thy Father who is in heaven. He used to say, The bold-faced are for Gehinnom, the shame-faced for the Garden of Eden. (He said further) May it be thy will, O Lord our God and God of our fathers, that the Temple be speedily rebuilt in our days, and grant our portion in thy Torah.

24. He used to say, At five years the age is reached for the study of the Scripture, at ten for the study of the

---

fleet as a hart. Cf. " I made haste, and delayed not, to observe Thy commandments " (Psalm 119. 60) ; see IV, 2.

thy Father who is in heaven. The term, " Our Father Who is in Heaven " or " My Father Who is in Heaven " is frequent in Rabbinic literature ; see p. 32.

bold-faced. The Heb. expression for "impudent" ; see the prayer of R. Judah the Prince, p. 26.

shame-faced. Those sensitive to public opinion. " Anyone who has a sense of shame will not readily sin " (Talmud).

Garden of Eden. The Heb. term for the abode of the righteous in the World to come.

may it be thy will. This prayer, added after the Amidah (p. 156), at one time closed Chapter v, and therefore the whole of Aboth. The remaining mishnas are later supplements.

24. The Ages of man—a favourite theme of all moralists. Leopold Löw, one of the great Jewish scholars of the nineteenth century, wrote a notable book on " The Ages of Man in Jewish Literature ". In this

לַמִּצְוֹת בֶּן־חָמֵשׁ עֶשְׂרֵה לַתַּלְמוּד בֶּן־שְׁמֹנֶה עֶשְׂרֵה לַחֻפָּה
בֶּן־עֶשְׂרִים לִרְדּוֹף בֶּן־שְׁלֹשִׁים לַכֹּחַ בֶּן־אַרְבָּעִים לַבִּינָה בֶּן־
חֲמִשִּׁים לָעֵצָה בֶּן־שִׁשִּׁים לְזִקְנָה בֶּן־שִׁבְעִים לְשֵׂיבָה בֶּן־
שְׁמוֹנִים לִגְבוּרָה בֶּן־תִּשְׁעִים לָשׁוּחַ בֶּן־מֵאָה כְּאִלּוּ מֵת וְעָבַר
וּבָטֵל מִן הָעוֹלָם : (כה) בֶּן־בַּג בַּג אוֹמֵר ׳ הֲפָךְ־בַּהּ וַהֲפָךְ־
בַּהּ דְּכֹלָּא בַּהּ וּבַהּ תֶּחֱזֵא וְסִיב וּבְלֵה בַהּ וּמִנַּהּ לָא תְזוּעַ
שֶׁאֵין לָךְ מִדָּה טוֹבָה הֵימֶנָּה : (כו) בֶּן־הֵא הֵא אוֹמֵר ׳
לְפֻם צַעֲרָא אַגְרָא :

רַבִּי חֲנַנְיָא בֶּן־עֲקַשְׁיָא וכו׳

post-Talmudic saying, man's life is divided into three periods—preparation, till twenty; activity, from twenty to sixty; and decline, from
sixty and beyond.

fulfilment of the commandments. See the introduction to the Bar
Mitzvah Prayer.

for seeking a livelihood. lit. "for pursuing". The "school-leaving"
age in this scheme of instruction is twenty. After five years of
Talmud study, he is free to devote himself to earning a livelihood.
During the first years of marriage, the student-husband usually lived
with, and was maintained by, his wife's parents.

thirty. The prime of physical vigour.

fifty. Based on the statement with regard to the Levites. On
reaching the age of fifty, they were considered as no longer fit for heavy
work, but continued to act as guides and counsellors to the younger
Levites (Numbers 8. 25f).

seventy. It was said of David, " he died in a good old age " (I Chronicles 29. 28), and he was seventy at his death.

strength. He must have possessed great natural strength and vigour
to have reached that age. Commentators refer to Psalm 90. 10. E. N.
Adler suggested that probably it is a euphemism (לְשׁוֹן סַגִּי נָהוֹר), and the
meaning is "increasing weakness". Such seems to have been the
opinion of Abraham Ibn Ezra, when in his poem on this theme he describes the man of eighty as a burden to himself and others.

he bends beneath the weight of years. lit. " to sink down"

hundred. The limit for a person to retain his faculties, and so
to be said at all as living.

Mishna, at thirteen for the fulfilment of the commandments, at fifteen for the study of the Talmud, at eighteen for marriage, at twenty for seeking a livelihood, at thirty for entering into one's full strength, at forty for understanding, at fifty for counsel, at sixty a man attains old age, at seventy the hoary head, at eighty the gift of special strength, at ninety he bends beneath the weight of years, at a hundred he is as if he were already dead and had passed away from the world.

25. Ben Bag Bag said, Turn it (the Torah) and turn it over again, for everything is in it, and contemplate it, and wax grey and old over it, and stir not from it, for thou canst have no better rule than this.

26. Ben Hai Hai said, According to the labour is the reward.

"Rabbi Chananya," etc., p. 27.

25. *Ben Bag Bag.* His full name was Yochanan ben Bag Bag. The latter name is said to indicate that he was a descendant of proselytes (בג בג is an abbreviation of *Ben Ger* and *Bath Ger*, " son of a proselyte " and " daughter of a proselyte "). An ingenious suggestion is that his name, and Ben Hai Hai, mentioned in the next mishna, belonged to the same man; and that he was the would-be proselyte who asked Hillel to teach him the whole Torah.

turn it. Study the Torah over and over again, study it from all sides.

everything is in it. It is a complete guide to life. " In it, without doubt, are history and tale ; proverb and enigma ; correction and wisdom ; knowledge and discretion ; poetry and word-play ; conviction and counsel : dirge, entreaty, prayer, praise, and every kind of supplication ; and all this in a Divine way superior to all the prolix benedictions in human books ; to say nothing of containing in its depths the Names of the Holy One, blessed is He, and secrets of being without end " (Lev Aboth).

wax grey and old over it. Do not think, on arriving at old age, that its guidance is no longer required.

stir not from it. Do not deviate from the path of life which it lays down ; or, do not leave if for extraneous studies.

rule. The Heb. may also denote "standard, or principle, of conduct ".

26. *according to the labour is the reward.* A popular proverb which is here applied to the Torah. What a man derives from it, is proportionate to the devotion he pays it. This and the preceding mishna are in Aramaic.

פֶּרֶק שִׁשִּׁי :

פרק קנין תורה או ברייתא דר' מאיר

כָּל־יִשְׂרָאֵל וכו'

שָׁנוּ חֲכָמִים בִּלְשׁוֹן הַמִּשְׁנָה בָּרוּךְ שֶׁבָּחַר בָּהֶם וּבְמִשְׁנָתָם :

(א) רַבִּי מֵאִיר אוֹמֵר · כָּל־הָעוֹסֵק בַּתּוֹרָה לִשְׁמָהּ זוֹכֶה לִדְבָרִים
הַרְבֵּה וְלֹא עוֹד אֶלָּא שֶׁכָּל־הָעוֹלָם כֻּלּוֹ כְּדַי הוּא לוֹ · נִקְרָא
רֵעַ אָהוּב אוֹהֵב אֶת־הַמָּקוֹם אוֹהֵב אֶת־הַבְּרִיּוֹת · וּמְלַבַּשְׁתּוֹ

CHAPTER VI.

ON THE ACQUISITION OF TORAH.

This chapter does not form part of the Sayings of the Fathers, or of the
canonical Mishna. When custom assigned a chapter of Aboth for the
Sabbaths between Passover and Pentecost, a reading was required for
the sixth Sabbath. This chapter was selected for the purpose, because
its contents harmonized so well with the spirit of Aboth. It opens with
a saying of R. Meir, and therefore came to be known as the " Boraitha
of Rabbi Meir ". *Boraitha* is the name for the teachings next in authority
to those that form part of the Mishna.

the sages, taught. In the Talmud this formula is in Aramaic, and
introduces a quotation from a source which has not been included in
the Mishna.

blessed be he. " He " most probably means God ; but some refer it
to any student who chooses this chapter for study, or to the compiler
who had " chosen " the ancient teachers and their words for his great
Eulogy on the Torah.

their Mishna. i.e. their teaching.

1. *Rabbi Meir.* Also known as Nehorai, is the most famous disciple
of Rabbi Akiba. Through his dialectical skill he attained eminence in
juristic discussion, and high place in the Sanhedrin. He was also
great as an exegete, and renowned as a fabulist. Among his teachings
are, " Scripture tells us (Deuteronomy 14. 1), *You are children of the
Lord your God*—whether we act as children should towards their Father,
or whether we do not, He ever remains our Father Who is in Heaven ".
Equally wonderful is his religious universalism. " Whence do we know
that even a heathen, if he obeys the Law of God, thereby attains the
same spiritual communion with God as the High Priest? Scripture
says (Leviticus 18. 5) ' Mine ordinances which if a man do, he
shall live by them '—it does not say, If priest, Levite, or Israelite do
God's ordinances, he shall attain life; but it says, if a *man* do them! "

VI

1

Sayings of the Fathers

"All Israel," etc., p. 13.

The sages taught the following in the style of the Mishna, —Blessed be he that made choice of them and their Mishna.

1. R. Meir said, Whosoever labours in the Torah for its own sake, merits many things ; and not only so, but the whole world is indebted to him : he is called friend, beloved, a lover of the All-present, a lover of mankind : it clothes him in meekness and reverence ; it fits him to become just,

Like his teacher Akiba, he preached the widest optimism. "And God saw everything that He had made, and, behold it was *very* good" (Genesis 1. 31). On this R. Meir's comment was, that even suffering, evil, nay, *death itself*, have a rightful and beneficent place in the Divine scheme. The following are examples of his maxims and parables. "Love thy friend who admonishes thee, and hate the one who flatters thee". "Man comes into the world with closed hands—ready to grasp at the world and its possessions. He departs with hands limp and open—he takes nothing with him ". Rabbi Meir was the husband of the wise Beruria ; see p. 588. He was a scribe by trade, and his life was full of trouble and misfortune. He died in his native city in Asia Minor. " Bury me by the sea shore ", was his last wish, " that the waves which wash the Land of my Fathers, may wash also my bones " ; see IV, 12 and 27, and concluding note to VI, p. 721.

whosoever labours in the Torah. Study of the Torah is a supreme religious duty ; see p. 15. And like every other religious duty, it must be pursued " for its own sake ".

for its own sake. From disinterested love, *lishmoh*, not for the sake of any profit or honour to be derived from it. The one true motive is the love of God. The doctrine of disinterested love of God and His Torah holds an important place in Rabbinical ethics, and has been called " the great creation of the Rabbis ". However, knowing human nature, they did not discourage doing right even from an imperfect motive, because it oftens ends in doing right for its own sake.

is indebted to him. Or, " he is deserving of the whole world ".

All-present. See on II, 14.

lover of mankind. The phrase used by Hillel (I, 12). He is no cloistered student who flees from his fellow-men, nor is he a cynic.

meekness. He walks humbly with God ; not ostentatiously, but with noiseless acts of love. The insistence on humility distinguishes Jewish, from Greek or pagan, ethics. A great Jewish philosopher declares, " Everything heroic in man is insignificant and perishable, and all his wisdom and virtue unable to stand the crucial test, unless they are the fruits of humility. In this regard there is no exception, neither for any man, any people, nor any age " (Hermann Cohen).

[105] *reverence.* Of God.

פרקי
אבות

ו

עֲנָוָה וְיִרְאָה וּמַכְשַׁרְתּוֹ לִהְיוֹת צַדִּיק חָסִיד יָשָׁר וְנֶאֱמָן
וּמְרַחַקְתּוֹ מִן־הַחֵטְא וּמְקָרַבְתּוֹ לִידֵי זְכוּת וְנֶהֱנִין מִמֶּנּוּ עֵצָה
וְתוּשִׁיָּה בִּינָה וּגְבוּרָה ׳ שֶׁנֶּאֱמַר לִי עֵצָה וְתוּשִׁיָּה אֲנִי בִינָה
לִי גְבוּרָה ׳ וְנוֹתֶנֶת לוֹ מַלְכוּת וּמֶמְשָׁלָה וְחִקּוּר דִּין וּמְגַלִּים
לוֹ רָזֵי תוֹרָה וְנַעֲשֶׂה כְּמַעְיָן שֶׁאֵינוֹ פוֹסֵק וּכְנָהָר שֶׁמִּתְגַּבֵּר
וְחוֹלֵה וְהֹוֶה צָנוּעַ וְאֶרֶךְ רוּחַ וּמוֹחֵל עַל־עֶלְבּוֹנוֹ וּמְגַדַּלְתּוֹ
וּמְרוֹמַמְתּוֹ עַל כָּל־הַמַּעֲשִׂים : (ב) אָמַר רַבִּי יְהוֹשֻׁעַ בֶּן־לֵוִי ׳
בְּכָל־יוֹם וָיוֹם בַּת־קוֹל יוֹצֵאת מֵהַר חוֹרֵב וּמַכְרֶזֶת וְאוֹמֶרֶת
אוֹי לָהֶם לַבְּרִיּוֹת מֵעֶלְבּוֹנָהּ שֶׁל־תּוֹרָה ׳ שֶׁכָּל־מִי שֶׁאֵינוֹ עוֹסֵק
בַּתּוֹרָה נִקְרָא נָזוּף ׳ שֶׁנֶּאֱמַר נֶזֶם זָהָב בְּאַף חֲזִיר אִשָּׁה יָפָה

virtue. lit. " merit ", *i.e.* conduct which earns him God's approval.

counsel is mine. The speaker is Wisdom, identified with Torah.

sovereignty and dominion. The general meaning is that knowledge of Torah endows one with a commanding personality. But the author has more particularly in mind, " By me (Torah) princes rule and nobles, even all the judges of the earth " (Proverbs 8. 16).

discerning judgment. This is based upon the last words of the verse.

secrets of the Torah are revealed. By God ; cf. " The counsel (lit. secret) of the Lord is with them that fear Him " (Psalm 25. 14).

a never-failing fountain. Cf. II, 11, where R. Elazar ben Arach is described as a " spring flowing with ever-sustained vigour ".

modest. The same word as in " walk humbly with thy God " (Micah 6. 8).

This mishna—which describes the perfect man as conceived by the Rabbis—enumerates the blessings that attend the study of the Torah, and the virtues which such study fosters in him who consecrates his days to it. To some people, the perfection of mind and soul presented in this mishna appears incomplete. Precious as the religious and ethical excellencies here given may be, they do not include physical qualities that made such a strong appeal to the ancient Greeks, as well as to many moderns. However, competent judges, both Jewish and non-Jewish, agree that the type of character described is both beautiful and saintly—a type of character produced by Rabbinism, and only by Rabbinism.

VI

2

Sayings of the Fathers

pious, upright and faithful ; it keeps him far from sin, and brings him near to virtue : through him the world enjoys counsel and sound knowledge, understanding and strength ; as it is said, Counsel is mine, and sound knowledge ; I am understanding ; I have strength : and it gives him sovereignty and dominion and discerning judgment : to him the secrets of the Torah are revealed ; he is made like a never-failing fountain, and like a river that flows on with ever-sustained vigour ; he becomes modest, patient, and forgiving of insults ; and it magnifies and exalts him above all things.

2. R. Joshua, the son of Levi, said, Every day a Bath-kol goes forth from Mount Sinai, proclaiming these words, Woe to mankind for contempt of the Torah, for whoever does not labour in the Torah is said to be under the divine censure ; as it is said, As a ring of gold in a swine's snout, so is a fair woman who turneth aside from discretion : and it says, And the tables were the work of

---

2. The Supreme Revelation of God is set at naught by neglect and ignorance. Such ignorance is a form of moral bondage.

Joshua, the son of Levi. A foremost exponent of the Haggadic element in Jewish lore, lived in the middle of the third century c.e.

Bath-kol. A heavenly voice. lit. " daughter of the voice ". This was held by many to be a form of Divine announcement to man in the later days when Prophecy had ceased.

Mount Sinai. Heb. " Mount Horeb ", the scene of the Revelation of the Torah.

mankind. Heb. *beriyyoth*, which denotes the whole human race. The Gentile world too suffers when the ethical teachings of the Torah are flouted.

contempt of the Torah. Manifested by the neglect of its study and practice.

under the divine censure. lit. " is called rebuked (*nazuf*) ".

as it is said. The proof-text is used to produce a *notarikon* (from Latin *notarius*, " a shorthand writer ") ; *i.e.* letters are selected to form the required word. Thus, *zaken* (old) is explained to mean *zeh shekonoh chochmah, i.e.* only he can be called *old* and entitled to all the respect due to the aged, who *has acquired wisdom*—irrespective of his years. These word-plays can be fully appreciated only by those familiar with the Hebrew original and with Rabbinic methods of exegesis.

פרקי
אבות

ו

וָסָרַת טָעַם : וְאוֹמֵר · וְהַלֻּחֹת מַעֲשֵׂה אֱלֹהִים הֵמָּה וְהַמִּכְתָּב
מִכְתַּב אֱלֹהִים הוּא חָרוּת עַל־הַלֻּחֹת · אַל־תִּקְרָא חָרוּת אֶלָּא
חֵרוּת שֶׁאֵין לְךָ בֶּן־חוֹרִין אֶלָּא מִי שֶׁעוֹסֵק בְּתַלְמוּד תּוֹרָה ·
וְכָל־מִי שֶׁעוֹסֵק בְּתַלְמוּד תּוֹרָה הֲרֵי זֶה מִתְעַלֶּה · שֶׁנֶּאֱמַר
וּמִמַּתָּנָה נַחֲלִיאֵל וּמִנַּחֲלִיאֵל בָּמוֹת : (נ) הַלּוֹמֵד מֵחֲבֵרוֹ פֶּרֶק
אֶחָד אוֹ הֲלָכָה אַחַת אוֹ פָסוּק אֶחָד אוֹ דִבּוּר אֶחָד אוֹ אֲפִילוּ
אוֹת אַחַת צָרִיךְ לִנְהָג בּוֹ כָּבוֹד · שֶׁכֵּן מָצִינוּ בְּדָוִד מֶלֶךְ
יִשְׂרָאֵל שֶׁלֹּא לָמַד מֵאֲחִיתֹפֶל אֶלָּא שְׁנֵי דְבָרִים בִּלְבָד קְרָאוֹ
רַבּוֹ אַלּוּפוֹ וּמְיֻדָּעוֹ · שֶׁנֶּאֱמַר וְאַתָּה אֱנוֹשׁ כְּעֶרְכִּי אַלּוּפִי וּמְיֻדָּעִי :
וַהֲלֹא דְבָרִים קַל וָחֹמֶר · וּמַה דָּוִד מֶלֶךְ יִשְׂרָאֵל שֶׁלֹּא לָמַד
מֵאֲחִיתֹפֶל אֶלָּא שְׁנֵי דְבָרִים בִּלְבָד קְרָאוֹ רַבּוֹ אַלּוּפוֹ וּמְיֻדָּעוֹ ·
הַלּוֹמֵד מֵחֲבֵרוֹ פֶּרֶק אֶחָד אוֹ הֲלָכָה אַחַת אוֹ פָסוּק אֶחָד אוֹ
דִבּוּר אֶחָד אוֹ אֲפִילוּ אוֹת אַחַת עַל־אַחַת כַּמָּה וְכַמָּה שֶׁצָּרִיךְ
לִנְהָג בּוֹ כָּבוֹד · וְאֵין כָּבוֹד אֶלָּא תוֹרָה · שֶׁנֶּאֱמַר כָּבוֹד חֲכָמִים

read not. A formula of Rabbinic exegesis. It does not imply a doubt as to the correctness of the Text. In this instance, only a change in a vowel is suggested to produce a fine homiletic thought.

no man is free. He alone is truly free who knows and obeys the laws of God. This is echoed in Milton's lines :

"Licence they mean when they cry Liberty ;
For who loves that, must first be wise and good."

Mattanah . . . Nachaliel . . . Bamoth. As words these place-names mean "gift, heritage of God, heights". The verse is thus interpreted : "From the gift of the Torah, man gains a Divine heritage, and that leads him to the heights of lofty ideals".

3. *a single chapter.* Of the Bible or Mishna. This does not mean the chapters into which the Text is now divided in printed Bibles. Those chapters are not older than the thirteenth century. The original division was more according to theme and subject matter.

rule. A statutory decision in Jewish Law.

verse. A section of Scripture shorter than a chapter. These go back to antiquity.

VI

3

Sayings of the Fathers

God, and the writing was the writing of God, graven upon the tables. Read not *charuth* (graven) but *cheruth* (freedom), for no man is free but he who labours in the Torah. But whosoever labours in the Torah, behold he shall be exalted, as it is said, And from Mattanah to Nachaliel, and from Nachaliel to Bamoth.

3. He who learns from his fellow a single chapter, a single rule, a single verse, a single expression, or even a single letter, ought to pay him honour; for so we find with David, King of Israel, who learnt only two things from Ahitophel, and yet regarded him as his master, his guide and his familiar friend, as it is said, But it was thou, a man, mine equal, my guide, and my familiar friend. Now, is it not an argument from minor to major? If David, the King of Israel, who learned only two things from Ahitophel, regarded him as his master, guide and familiar friend, how much more ought one who learns from his fellow a chapter, rule, verse, expression, or even a single letter, to pay him honour? And honour is nothing but Torah; as it is said,

expression. A Biblical or Mishna saying.

letter. In the case of a word concerning which there is a doubt in regard to spelling.

only two things. The word *only* is puzzling, so is the peculiar argument. Commentators differ as to the two things which David learnt from Ahitophel, and their explanations are forced. Joseph Jaaḅez (fifteenth century), Midrash Shemuel (sixteenth century) and Chaim Walosin (nineteenth century) remarked on the logical incoherence of the reasoning. However, by a simple emendation, *shne debarim*, "two things", become one word, *shenidbarim*, which yields the meaning, "who only conversed together". According to the amended text, the reasoning is plain. If David the King showed honour to one of his subjects from whom he learnt nothing, but merely conversed with him, how much more is it the duty of an ordinary person to show honour to an equal from whom he *has* learnt aught of Torah. Strack, Oesterley, and Herford endorse the emendation, and declare that in this way all difficulties disappear; see Hertz, *Sermons* III, p. 261–265.

and my familiar friend. The next verse continues; " we took sweet counsel together " (Psalm 55. 15).

argument from minor to major. The first of the thirteen exegetical rules of Rabbi Ishmael, p. 42.

וַ יִנְחֲלוּ וּתְמִימִים יִנְחֲלוּ טוֹב ' וְאֵין טוֹב אֶלָּא תוֹרָה ' שֶׁנֶּאֱמַר
כִּי לֶקַח טוֹב נָתַתִּי לָכֶם תּוֹרָתִי אַל־תַּעֲזֹבוּ : (ו) כַּךְ הִיא
דַּרְכָּהּ שֶׁל־תּוֹרָה ' פַּת בְּמֶלַח תֹּאכֵל וּמַיִם בִּמְשׂוּרָה תִשְׁתֶּה
וְעַל הָאָרֶץ תִּישָׁן וְחַיֵּי צַעַר תִּחְיֶה וּבַתּוֹרָה אַתָּה עָמֵל ' אִם־
אַתָּה עֹשֶׂה כֵּן אַשְׁרֶיךָ וְטוֹב לָךְ ' אַשְׁרֶיךָ בָּעוֹלָם הַזֶּה וְטוֹב
לָךְ לָעוֹלָם הַבָּא : (ה) אַל־תְּבַקֵּשׁ גְּדֻלָּה לְעַצְמֶךָ וְאַל־תַּחְמֹד
כָּבוֹד ' יוֹתֵר מִלִּמּוּדְךָ עֲשֵׂה ' וְאַל־תִּתְאַוֶּה לְשֻׁלְחָנָם שֶׁל־מְלָכִים '
שֶׁשֻּׁלְחָנְךָ גָּדוֹל מִשֻּׁלְחָנָם וְכִתְרְךָ גָּדוֹל מִכִּתְרָם ' וְנֶאֱמָן הוּא
בַּעַל מְלַאכְתְּךָ שֶׁיְּשַׁלֵּם לָךְ שְׂכַר פְּעֻלָּתֶךָ : (ו) גְּדוֹלָה תוֹרָה
יוֹתֵר מִן־הַכְּהֻנָּה וּמִן־הַמַּלְכוּת ' שֶׁהַמַּלְכוּת נִקְנֵית בִּשְׁלֹשִׁים
מַעֲלוֹת וְהַכְּהֻנָּה בְּעֶשְׂרִים וְאַרְבַּע וְהַתּוֹרָה נִקְנֵית בְּאַרְבָּעִים
וּשְׁמוֹנָה דְּבָרִים ' וְאֵלּוּ הֵן ' בְּתַלְמוּד בִּשְׁמִיעַת הָאֹזֶן ' בַּעֲרִיכַת

4. *this is the way.* Such is what may have to be endured by those who devote themselves to its study. This is asceticism, and the ascetic note is rare in Jewish literature. Judaism preached self-control, and not refusal to make moderate use of the good things in life; see mishna 8.

morsel of bread with salt. Mentioned in the Talmud as the meal of the poor.

of hardship. Or, " of privation ".

the while thou toilest in the Torah. Devoting most of his energies to study, he earns only enough for his barest necessities. A man with means, on the other hand, was not expected to impoverish himself and live an ascetic life, while pursuing study.

happy shalt thou be. As in IV, 1.

5. On unworldly ambition.

seek not greatness for thyself. Cf. I, 10.

let thy deeds exceed thy learning. Cf. I, 17 ; III, 12.

table of kings. Laden though it be with costly foods.

thy table is greater than theirs. Because it is hallowed by the conversation on sacred themes ; see III, 4.

thy crown. Of the Torah (IV, 17). By his unworldly devotion to the Torah, the pious increases reverence for it among men, and thus spreads true religion and morality. Such a one is free from all lust for personal glory and reputation (Beer).

VI

4-6

Sayings of the Fathers

The wise shall inherit honour ; and the perfect shall inherit good. And good is nothing but Torah ; as it is said, For I give you good doctrine, forsake ye not my Torah.

4. This is the way that is becoming for the study of the Torah : a morsel of bread with salt thou must eat, and water by measure thou must drink ; thou must sleep upon the ground, and live a life of trouble the while thou toilest in the Torah. If thou doest thus, Happy shalt thou be, and it shall be well with thee ; happy shalt thou be—in this world, and it shall be well with thee—in the world to come.

5. Seek not greatness for thyself, and court not honour ; let thy deeds exceed thy learning ; and crave not after the table of kings ; for thy table is greater than theirs, and thy crown is greater than theirs, and thy Employer is faithful to pay thee the reward of thy work.

6. The Torah is greater than the priesthood and than royalty, seeing that royalty demands thirty qualifications, the priesthood twenty-four, while the Torah is acquired by forty-eight. And these are they : [1]By audible study ; by distinct pronunciation ; by understanding and discernment of the heart ; [5]by awe, reverence, meekness, cheerfulness ;

---

6. The Student of Religion.

demands thirty qualifications. Enumerated in tractate Sanhedrin ; while those of the priesthood are deduced from Numbers 18. 8f.

[1]*audible study.* lit. " study with hearing of the ear ". Silent meditation would not leave the same imprint on the memory.

distinct pronunciation. Rehearsing the lessons aloud ; the characteristic method of Torah-study among Jews.

understanding. See on III, 21 ; and on the wider meaning of "heart," II, 13.

discernment of the heart. Indicates a mind capable of grasping ideas, and drawing fine distinctions.

[5]*awe.* In the disciple's attitude towards his master.

reverence. Of God, on the principle that " fear (reverence) of the Lord is the beginning of wisdom " ; .Psalm 111. 10.

meekness. See on VI, 1.

cheerfulness. In the performance of the commandments—*simchah shel mitzvah.*

שְׂפָתַיִם · בְּבִינַת חַלֵב בְּשִׂפּוּל הַלֵּב · בְּאֵימָה · בְּיִרְאָה ·
בַּעֲנָוָה · בְּשִׂמְחָה · בְּשִׁמּוּשׁ חֲכָמִים · בְּדִבּוּק חֲבֵרִים · בְּפִלְפּוּל
הַתַּלְמִידִים · בְּיִשּׁוּב · בְּמִקְרָא וּבְמִשְׁנָה · בְּמִעוּט סְחוֹרָה ·
בְּמִעוּט דֶּרֶךְ אֶרֶץ · בְּמִעוּט תַּעֲנוּג · בְּמִעוּט שֵׁנָה · בְּמִעוּט
שִׂיחָה · בְּמִעוּט שְׂחוֹק · בְּאֹרֶךְ אַפַּיִם · בְּלֶב־טוֹב · בֶּאֱמוּנַת
חֲכָמִים · בְּקַבָּלַת הַיִּסּוּרִים · הַמַּכִּיר אֶת־מְקוֹמוֹ · וְהַשָּׂמֵחַ
בְּחֶלְקוֹ · וְהָעוֹשֶׂה סְיָג לִדְבָרָיו · וְאֵינוֹ מַחֲזִיק טוֹבָה לְעַצְמוֹ ·
אָהוּב · אוֹהֵב אֶת־הַמָּקוֹם · אוֹהֵב אֶת־הַבְּרִיּוֹת · אוֹהֵב אֶת־
הַצְּדָקוֹת · אוֹהֵב אֶת־הַמֵּישָׁרִים · אוֹהֵב אֶת־הַתּוֹכָחוֹת ·
וּמִתְרַחֵק מִן־הַכָּבוֹד · וְלֹא־מֵגִיס לִבּוֹ בְּתַלְמוּדוֹ · וְאֵינוֹ שָׂמֵחַ
בְּהוֹרָאָה · נוֹשֵׂא בְעֹל עִם־חֲבֵרוֹ · וּמַכְרִיעוֹ לְכַף זְכוּת ·
וּמַעֲמִידוֹ עַל־הָאֱמֶת · וּמַעֲמִידוֹ עַל־הַשָּׁלוֹם · וּמִתְיַשֵּׁב

---

ministering to the sages. Heb. *shimmush*; close personal contact
with an officiating Rabbi in order to learn religious practice.

¹⁰*attaching oneself to colleagues.* Studying with other disciples, and
not alone; cf. I, 6.

sedateness. Calm and deliberate approach to study.

Scripture . . . Mishna. The essential foundation upon which
Jewish religious knowledge is based. Ignorance of either disqualifies a
teacher.

moderation in business. Cf. II, 6; IV, 12.

¹⁵*intercourse with the world.* Heb. *derech eretz* (II, 2).

pleasure. Cf. VI, 4.

sleep. See III, 14.

laughter. Cf. III, 17.

²⁰*patience.* An indispensable requirement in all intellectual work.

good heart. Cf. II, 18.

faith in the wise. Confidence in the soundness of their instruction.

resignation under affliction. His sufferings do not weaken his faith in
God and his devotion to the Torah. He realizes that the heart is purified,
and the character uplifted, by sorrow; and that, far from being a sign of
God's displeasure, affliction may be a proof of God's love (יִסּוּרִין שֶׁל אַהֲבָה).

VI

6

Sayings of the Fathers

by ministering to the sages, [10]by attaching oneself to colleagues, by discussion with pupils; by sedateness; by knowledge of the Scripture and of the Mishna; by moderation in business, [15]in intercourse with the world, in pleasure, in sleep, in conversation, in laughter; [20]by patience; by a good heart; by faith in the wise; by resignation under affliction; by recognising one's place, [25]rejoicing in one's portion, putting a fence to one's words, claiming no merit for oneself; by being beloved, loving the All-present, [30]loving mankind, loving just courses, rectitude and reproof; by keeping oneself far from honour; not boasting of one's learning, [35]nor delighting in giving decisions; by bearing the yoke with one's fellow, judging him favourably, and leading him to truth and peace; by [40]being composed in one's study;

Therefore must affliction be received in resignation; and the true Israelite blesses the Name of God for weal and for woe; see p. 87.

recognizing one's place. Inducing in him a spirit of humility. Cf. III, 1; IV, 4.

[25]*rejoicing in one's portion.* He is *happy* in his vocation, despite the privations of a student's life.

putting a fence to one's words. Cf. " Ye sages, be heedful of your words " (I, 11).

claiming no merit for oneself. Cf. II, 9.

being beloved. His character arouses affection in his fellow men; see III, 13.

loving the All-present. Only by loving the Giver of the Torah can he love the Torah itself.

[30]*loving mankind.* For this and the preceding two phrases, see VI, 1.

rectitude. Uprightness.

and reproof. Derived from Proverbs 9. 8, " Reprove a wise man, and he will love thee ".

far from honour. He shuns worldly fame.

not boasting of one's learning. One of the tests of humility. " Let another man praise thee, and not thine own mouth " (Proverbs 27. 2).

[35]*nor delighting in giving decisions.* Cf. IV, 9.

yoke with one's fellow. He can work *with* others, and helps his fellow in the acquisition of Torah and the performance of its duties.

judging him favourably. lit. " in the scale of merit "; see I, 6.

leading him to truth and peace. By helping his colleague to arrive at a just decision, not only is truth vindicated but peace is promoted.

[40]*composed in one's teaching.* He is calm and deliberate when imparting instruction.

בְּתַלְמוּדוֹ · שׁוֹאֵל · וּמֵשִׁיב · שׁוֹמֵעַ וּמוֹסִיף · הַלּוֹמֵד עַל־מְנָת
לְלַמֵּד · וְהַלּוֹמֵד עַל־מְנָת לַעֲשׂוֹת · הַמַּחְכִּים אֶת־רַבּוֹ · וְהַמְכַוֵּן
אֶת־שְׁמוּעָתוֹ · וְהָאוֹמֵר דָּבָר בְּשֵׁם אוֹמְרוֹ · הָא לָמַדְתָּ כָּל־
הָאוֹמֵר דָּבָר בְּשֵׁם אוֹמְרוֹ מֵבִיא גְאֻלָּה לָעוֹלָם · שֶׁנֶּאֱמַר וַתֹּאמֶר
אֶסְתֵּר לַמֶּלֶךְ בְּשֵׁם מָרְדֳּכָי : (ז) גְּדוֹלָה תוֹרָה שֶׁהִיא נוֹתֶנֶת
חַיִּים לְעוֹשֶׂיהָ בָּעוֹלָם הַזֶּה וּבָעוֹלָם הַבָּא · שֶׁנֶּאֱמַר כִּי־חַיִּים
הֵם לְמֹצְאֵיהֶם וּלְכָל־בְּשָׂרוֹ מַרְפֵּא · וְאוֹמֵר רִפְאוּת תְּהִי לְשָׁרֶּךָ
וְשִׁקּוּי לְעַצְמוֹתֶיךָ · וְאוֹמֵר עֵץ־חַיִּים הִיא לַמַּחֲזִיקִים בָּהּ
וְתֹמְכֶיהָ מְאֻשָּׁר · וְאוֹמֵר כִּי לִוְיַת חֵן הֵם לְרֹאשֶׁךָ וַעֲנָקִים
לְגַרְגְּרֹתֶךָ · וְאוֹמֵר תִּתֵּן לְרֹאשֶׁךָ לִוְיַת־חֵן עֲטֶרֶת תִּפְאֶרֶת
תְּמַגְּנֶךָּ · וְאוֹמֵר כִּי בִי יִרְבּוּ יָמֶיךָ וְיוֹסִיפוּ לְךָ שְׁנוֹת חַיִּים ·
וְאוֹמֵר אֹרֶךְ יָמִים בִּימִינָהּ בִּשְׂמֹאולָהּ עֹשֶׁר וְכָבוֹד · וְאוֹמֵר
כִּי אֹרֶךְ יָמִים וּשְׁנוֹת חַיִּים וְשָׁלוֹם יוֹסִיפוּ לָךְ : (ח) רַבִּי

asking and answering. To be understood as in v, 10, " he questions according to the subject matter, and answers to the point ".

adding thereto. The same word as in " he who does not increase his knowledge, decreases it " (I, 13).

⁴ ⁵*teaching . . . practising.* See IV, 6.

making one's master wiser. On the principle expressed in the saying of Rabbi Judah the Prince, " Much have I learned from my teachers, more from my colleagues, and most of all from my pupils ".

fixing attention upon his discourse. Since instruction was oral, it was of the utmost importance that the pupil should have an exact report of it in his memory, otherwise he would transmit it to others in an inaccurate version.

in the name of. Unless he did so, he would be credited with a statement which he had not originated, and it would be " *stealing* the good opinion of men ". Verify your citations, and acknowledge your indebtedness to your sources—is the counsel to modern students.

in the name of Mordecai. The fact that Mordecai's name had been mentioned in Esther's report of the plot to assassinate the king, had a

by asking and answering, hearing and adding thereto; by learning with the object of teaching, and [45]by learning with the object of practising ; by making one's master wiser, fixing attention upon his discourse, and reporting a thing in the name of him who said it. So thou hast learnt, Whosoever reports a thing in the name of him that said it brings deliverance into the world; as it is said, And Esther told the king in the name of Mordecai.

7. Great is the Torah which gives life to those that practise it in this world and in the world to come, as it is said, For they are life unto those that find them, and health to all their flesh ; and it says, It shall be health to thy navel, and marrow to thy bones ; and it says, It is a tree of life to them that grasp it, and of them that uphold it every one is rendered happy ; and it says, For they shall be a chaplet of grace unto thy head, and chains about thy neck ; and it says, It shall give to thine head a chaplet of grace; a crown of glory it shall deliver to thee ; and it says, For by me thy days shall be multiplied, and the years of thy life shall be increased ; and it says, Length of days is in its right hand ; in its left hand are riches and honour ; and it says, For length of days, and years of life, and peace shall they add to thee.

determining influence upon subsequent events; Esther 6. 2f. It led to the fall of Haman, and the salvation of the Jews in Persia.

This mishna, a continuation of the panegyric in praise of Torah in the opening mishna of this chapter, gives in essence the noblest ethical ideals of Aboth. Alongside the formal qualifications of the student—which shows how serious and sacred a thing was religious study to the Rabbis of old—" magnanimous " virtues are proclaimed as essential qualities, and these are such as are to be desired by all men, whatever their creed. Among these qualities are, love of God and man, cheerfulness, love of mercy, truthfulness, humility, peacefulness ; in a word, " a good heart " (II, 9).

7. A continuation of the theme in the preceding mishna.

they are life. Referring to the words of wisdom, *i.e.* Torah. Similarly in the other quotations from Proverbs, Wisdom and Torah are identified.

פרקי
אבות

שִׁמְעוֹן בֶּן־יְהוּדָה מִשֵּׁם רַבִּי שִׁמְעוֹן בֶּן־יוֹחַי אוֹמֵר · הַנּוֹי

וְהַכֹּחַ וְהָעשֶׁר וְהַכָּבוֹד וְהַחָכְמָה וְהַזִּקְנָה וְהַשֵּׂיבָה וְהַבָּנִים

נָאֶה לַצַּדִּיקִים וְנָאֶה לָעוֹלָם · שֶׁנֶּאֱמַר עֲטֶרֶת תִּפְאֶרֶת שֵׂיבָה

בְּדֶרֶךְ צְדָקָה תִּמָּצֵא · וְאוֹמֵר תִּפְאֶרֶת בַּחוּרִים כֹּחָם וַהֲדַר

זְקֵנִים שֵׂיבָה · וְאוֹמֵר עֲטֶרֶת חֲכָמִים עָשְׁרָם · וְאוֹמֵר עֲטֶרֶת

זְקֵנִים בְּנֵי בָנִים וְתִפְאֶרֶת בָּנִים אֲבוֹתָם · וְאוֹמֵר וְחָפְרָה

הַלְּבָנָה וּבוֹשָׁה הַחַמָּה כִּי־מָלַךְ יְיָ צְבָאוֹת בְּהַר צִיּוֹן וּבִירוּשָׁלַם

וְנֶגֶד זְקֵנָיו כָּבוֹד : רַבִּי שִׁמְעוֹן בֶּן־מְנַסְיָא אוֹמֵר · אֵלּוּ שֶׁבַע

מִדּוֹת שֶׁמָּנוּ חֲכָמִים לַצַּדִּיקִים כֻּלָּם נִתְקַיְּמוּ בְּרַבִּי וּבְבָנָיו :

(ט) אָמַר רַבִּי יוֹסֵי בֶּן־קִסְמָא · פַּעַם אַחַת הָיִיתִי מְהַלֵּךְ בַּדֶּרֶךְ

וּפָגַע בִּי אָדָם אֶחָד וְנָתַן־לִי שָׁלוֹם וְהֶחֱזַרְתִּי לוֹ שָׁלוֹם · אָמַר

לִי · רַבִּי מֵאֵי־זֶה מָקוֹם אָתָּה · אָמַרְתִּי לוֹ·מֵעִיר גְּדוֹלָה שֶׁל־

חֲכָמִים וְשֶׁל־סוֹפְרִים אָנִי · אָמַר לִי · רַבִּי רְצוֹנְךָ שֶׁתָּדוּר עִמָּנוּ

בִּמְקוֹמֵנוּ וַאֲנִי אֶתֵּן לְךָ אֶלֶף אֲלָפִים דִּינְרֵי זָהָב וַאֲבָנִים טוֹבוֹת

וּמַרְגָּלִיּוֹת · אָמַרְתִּי לוֹ·אִם אַתָּה נוֹתֵן לִי כָּל־כֶּסֶף וְזָהָב וַאֲבָנִים

טוֹבוֹת וּמַרְגָּלִיּוֹת שֶׁבָּעוֹלָם אֵינִי דָר אֶלָּא בִּמְקוֹם תּוֹרָה · וְכֵן

כָּתוּב בְּסֵפֶר תְּהִלִּים עַל־יְדֵי דָוִד מֶלֶךְ יִשְׂרָאֵל· טוֹב לִי תוֹרַת

---

8. *Simeon, the son of Judah.* A disciple of R. Simeon ben Yochai
(III, 4; IV, 17). This mishna presents the life of the righteous under an
aspect quite different from that in mishna 4.

beauty . . . children. Eight adornments are enumerated, whereas
the number is given as seven at the end of the paragraph. Elijah, the
Gaon of Wilna, omits " wisdom ", because it is not referred to in the
Biblical quotations. The Palestinian Talmud omits " old age ".

Simeon, the son of Menasya. Contemporary of R. Simeon ben Judah.
9. The incomparable worth of the Torah.

José, the son of Kisma. Colleague of R. Chananya ben Teradyon
(III, 8). He did not join in the revolt under Bar Cochba, and remained
undisturbed by the Roman authorities in the terrible persecutions that

VI

8. R. Simeon, the son of Judah, in the name of R. Simeon, the son of Yochai, said, Beauty, strength, riches, honour, wisdom, (old age,) a hoary head, and children, are comely to the righteous and comely to the world ; as it is said, The hoary head is a crown of glory, if it be found in the way of righteousness ; and it says, The glory of young men is their strength, and the adornment of old men is the hoary head ; and it says, A crown unto the wise is their riches ; and it says, Children's children are the crown of old men, and the adornment of children are their fathers ; and it is said, Then the moon shall be confounded and the sun ashamed ; for the Lord of hosts shall reign in Mount Zion and in Jerusalem, and before his elders shall be glory.

R. Simeon, the son of Menasya, said, These seven qualifications which the sages enumerated as becoming to the righteous, were all realised in Rabbi Judah the Prince, and in his sons.

9. R. José, the son of Kisma, said, I was once walking by the way, when a man met me and greeted me, and I returned his greeting. He said to me, Rabbi, from what place art thou ? I said to him, I come from a great city of sages and scribes. He said to me, If thou art willing to dwell with us in our place, I will give thee a thousand thousand golden dinars and precious stones and pearls. I said to him, Wert thou to give me all the silver and gold and precious stones and pearls in the world, I would not dwell anywhere but in a home of the Torah ; and thus it is written in the

---

followed. His saying is the only personal experience related in the first person in the six chapters (I, 17 is only an apparent exception).

greeted me. lit. " gave me peace ". The Jewish greeting is *sholom aleychem*, " Peace be unto thee " ; and the reply is *aleychem sholom*, " unto thee be peace ".

great city. Probably Yavneh.

willing to dwell with us. The man was anxious to secure the Rabbi as a teacher to his community. The phrase, " a thousand thousand golden dinars " is equivalent to, " Ask whatever you wish ".

home of the Torah. As in IV, 18. José was evidently not the *born* teacher or missionary ; he was purely the student and scholar type.

פָּיךְ מֵאַלְפֵי זָהָב וָכָסֶף · וְלֹא עֹוד אֶלָּא שֶׁבִּשְׁעַת פְּטִירָתוֹ שֶׁל־
אָדָם אֵין מְלַוִּים לוֹ לָאָדָם לֹא כֶסֶף וְלֹא זָהָב וְלֹא אֲבָנִים טֹובֹות
וּמַרְגָּלִיֹות אֶלָּא תֹורָה וּמַעֲשִׂים טֹובִים בִּלְבָד · שֶׁנֶּאֱמַר
בְּהִתְהַלֶּכְךָ תַּנְחֶה אֹתָךְ בְּשָׁכְבְּךָ תִּשְׁמֹר עָלֶיךָ וַהֲקִיצֹותָ הִיא
תְשִׂיחֶךָ · בְּהִתְהַלֶּכְךָ תַּנְחֶה אֹתָךְ בָּעֹולָם הַזֶּה בְּשָׁכְבְּךָ
תִּשְׁמֹור עָלֶיךָ בַּקֶּבֶר וַהֲקִיצֹותָ הִיא תְשִׂיחֶךָ לָעֹולָם הַבָּא ·
וְאֹומֵר לִי הַכֶּסֶף וְלִי הַזָּהָב נְאֻם יְיָ צְבָאֹות : (י) חֲמִשָּׁה
קִנְיָנִים קָנָה לֹו הַקָּדֹוש בָּרוּךְ הוּא בְּעֹולָמֹו וְאֵלּוּ הֵן · תֹורָה
קִנְיָן אֶחָד שָׁמַיִם וָאָרֶץ קִנְיָן אֶחָד אַבְרָהָם קִנְיָן אֶחָד יִשְׂרָאֵל
קִנְיָן אֶחָד בֵּית הַמִּקְדָּש קִנְיָן אֶחָד : תֹורָה מִנַּיִן · דִּכְתִיב יְיָ
קָנָנִי רֵאשִׁית דַּרְכֹּו קֶדֶם מִפְעָלָיו מֵאָז : שָׁמַיִם וָאָרֶץ מִנַּיִן ·
דִּכְתִיב כֹּה אָמַר יְיָ הַשָּׁמַיִם כִּסְאִי וְהָאָרֶץ הֲדֹם רַגְלָי אֵי־זֶה
בַיִת אֲשֶׁר תִּבְנוּ־לִי וְאֵי־זֶה מָקֹום מְנוּחָתִי · וְאֹומֵר מָה רַבּוּ
מַעֲשֶׂיךָ יְיָ כֻּלָּם בְּחָכְמָה עָשִׂיתָ מָלְאָה הָאָרֶץ קִנְיָנֶךָ : אַבְרָהָם

---

the silver is mine. The meaning is : All the treasures of the world
are at God's disposal. If He wills me to share in them, He will bestow
them upon me while I reside in the home of the Torah.

10. An anonymous number-saying, like those in Chapter v. It
is included here because the Torah is one of the special Possessions
mentioned herein.

made especially his own. While He created the universe in its entirety,
the claim is made in Rabbinic literature that there are certain things
which " He made especially His own ". In one version, the number is
three : Torah, Israel and the Sanctuary ; here, " Abraham " and
" heaven and earth " are added. Nowhere else is the total increased to
five.

Abraham. The Gaon of Wilna deleted the word, since the corres-
ponding proof-text (see below) is not suitable.

VI

10

*Sayings
of the
Fathers*

Book of Psalms by the hands of David, King of Israel, The law of thy mouth is better unto me than thousands of gold and silver ; and not only so, but in the hour of man's departure neither silver nor gold nor precious stones nor pearls accompany him, but only Torah and good works, as it is said, When thou walkest it shall lead thee ; when thou liest down it shall watch over thee ; and when thou awakest it shall talk with thee :—when thou walkest it shall lead thee— in this world ; when thou liest down it shall watch over thee—in the grave ; and when thou awakest it shall talk with thee—in the world to come. And it says, The silver is mine, and the gold is mine, saith the Lord of hosts.

10. Five possessions the Holy One, blessed be he, made especially his own in his world, and these are they, The Torah, heaven and earth, Abraham, Israel, and the Holy Temple. Whence know we this of the Torah ? Because it is written, The Lord possessed me as the beginning of his way, before his works, from of old. Whence of heaven and earth ? Because it is written, Thus saith the Lord, The heaven is my throne, and the earth is my footstool : what manner of house will ye build unto me ? and what manner of place for my rest ? and it says, How manifold are thy works, O Lord ! In wisdom hast thou made them all : the earth is full of thy possessions. Whence of Abraham ? Because it is written, And he blessed him, and said, Blessed be Abram of the Most High God, Master of heaven and earth. Whence of Israel ? Because it is written, Till thy people pass over, O Lord, till the people pass over which thou hast acquired ; and it says, As for

---

possessed me. Wisdom, *i.e.* Torah.

how manifold are thy works. A second text is added, because it includes the keyword " possession ", which is absent in the first.

and he blessed him. According to the Gaon of Wilna, this provides a third proof-text for " heaven and earth " as a " possession ".

מִנַּיִן · דִּכְתִיב וַיְבָרֲכֵהוּ וַיֹּאמַר בָּרוּךְ אַבְרָם לְאֵל עֶלְיוֹן קֹנֵה
שָׁמַיִם וָאָרֶץ : יִשְׂרָאֵל מִנַּיִן · דִּכְתִיב עַד־יַעֲבֹר עַמְּךָ יְיָ עַד־
יַעֲבֹר עַם־זוּ קָנִיתָ · וְאוֹמֵר לִקְדוֹשִׁים אֲשֶׁר־בָּאָרֶץ הֵמָּה וְאַדִּירֵי
כָּל־חֶפְצִי בָם : בֵּית הַמִּקְדָּשׁ מִנַּיִן · דִּכְתִיב מָכוֹן לְשִׁבְתְּךָ
פָּעַלְתָּ יְיָ מִקְדָּשׁ אֲדֹנָי כּוֹנְנוּ יָדֶיךָ · וְאוֹמֵר וַיְבִיאֵם אֶל־גְּבוּל
קָדְשׁוֹ הַר זֶה קָנְתָה יְמִינוֹ : (יא) כֹּל מַה־שֶּׁבָּרָא הַקָּדוֹשׁ בָּרוּךְ
הוּא בְּעוֹלָמוֹ לֹא בְרָאוֹ אֶלָא לִכְבוֹדוֹ · שֶׁנֶּאֱמַר כֹּל הַנִּקְרָא
בִשְׁמִי וְלִכְבוֹדִי בְּרָאתִיו יְצַרְתִּיו אַף עֲשִׂיתִיו : וְאוֹמֵר · יְיָ ׀
יִמְלֹךְ לְעֹלָם וָעֶד :

רַבִּי חֲנַנְיָא בֶּן־עֲקַשְׁיָא וכו'

---

    the saints. lit. " holy ones ", denoting Israel as the people hallowed
by the Torah, and sanctified by its commandments.

    11. *whatsoever the Holy One, blessed be he, created.* This final para-
graph supplements the preceding. Not only the things there specified
were created by God for His purpose. The *whole* universe is a witness
to God's greatness and glory, and the Selection of Israel was for the
accomplishment of a design which embraced the entire human race ;
viz., the acknowledgment of the Divine Sovereignty by all His creatures.
In the Prayer Book, this sublime aspiration is uttered at the conclusion
of each Service, when the verse, " The Lord shall reign for ever and
ever ", is followed by the Prophet's declaration : " The Lord shall be
King over all the earth ; in that day shall the Lord be One, and His
name One " ; (see p. 210).

the saints that are in the earth, they are the noble ones in whom is all my delight.   Whence of the Holy Temple ? Because it is written, The place, O Lord, which thou hast made for thee to dwell in, the sanctuary, O Lord, which thy hands have prepared ; and it says, And he brought them to the border of his sanctuary, to this mountain which his might had acquired.

11. Whatsoever the Holy One, blessed be he, created in his world he created but for his glory, as it is said, Everything that is called by my Name, it is for my glory I have created it, I have formed it, yea, I have made it ; and it says, The Lord shall reign for ever and ever.

"Rabbi Chananya," etc., p. 27.

OLEYNU. The reading of one of the chapters of Aboth in the synagogue precedes Oleynu and Mourner's Kaddish in the Sabbath Afternoon Service.

In many manuscripts of Aboth, as well as in early editions, there are additional endings, either in this chapter or the preceding one. The most beautiful of these, and especially appropriate because chapter vi opens with a saying of Rabbi Meir, is the following: "When Rabbi Meir concluded the reading of the Book of Job, he said, ' It is the destiny of man to die, and of cattle to be slaughtered; and all are doomed to death. Happy is he who was reared in Torah, and who toils in Torah ; who by his life causes joy of spirit to his Maker ; who advances in good repute, and departs this world with a good name " (Talmud).

From the Jewish Moralists

1. THE PATHS OF LIFE

—ELIEZER BEN ISAAC *(10th century)*

My son, give God all honor and the gratitude which is His due
Thou hast need of Him, but He needs thee not. Put no trust in
thy mere physical well-being here below. Many a one has lain down
to sleep at nightfall, but at morn has not risen again. See that thou
guard well thy soul's holiness; let the thought of thy heart be
saintly, and profane not thy soul with words of impurity.

Visit the sick and suffering man, and let thy countenance be
cheerful when he sees it, but not so that thou oppress the helpless
one with gaiety. Comfort those that are in grief; let piety where
thou seest it affect thee even to tears; and then it may be that thou
wilt be spared the grief of weeping over the death of thy children.

Respect the poor man by gifts whose hands he knows not of;
be not deaf to his beseechings, deal not hard words out to him. From
a wicked neighbor, see that thou keep aloof, and spend not much of
thy time among the people who speak ill of their brother-man; be
not as the fly that is always seeking sick and wounded places; and
tell not of the faults and failings of those about thee.

Take no one to wife unworthy to be thy life's partner, and keep
thy sons close to the study of Divine things. Dare not to rejoice
when thine enemy comes to the ground; but give him food when he
hungers. Be on thy guard lest thou give pain ever to the widow and
the orphan; and beware lest thou ever set thyself up to be both witness and judge against another.

Never enter thy house with abrupt and startling step, and bear
not thyself so that those who dwell under thy roof shall dread when
in thy presence. Purge thy soul of angry passion, that inheritance of [122]

fools; love wise men, and strive to know more and more of the works and the ways of the Creator.

2. *From* THE ETHICAL WILL

—ASHER BEN YECHIEL *(13th century)*

From the Jewish Moralists

Be not ready to quarrel; avoid oaths and passionate adjurations, excess of laughter and outbursts of wrath; they disturb and confound the reason of man. Avoid all dealings wherein there is a lie; and make not gold the foremost longing of thy life; for that is the first step to idolatry. Rather give money than words; and as to ill words, see that thou place them in the scale of understanding before they leave thy lips.

What has been uttered in thy presence, even though not told as secret, let it not pass from thee to others. And if one tell thee a tale, say not to him that thou has heard it all before. Do not fix thine eyes too much on one who is far above thee in wealth, but on those who are behind thee in worldy fortune.

Put no one to open shame; misuse not thy power against any one; who can tell whether thou wilt not some day be powerless thyself?

Do not struggle vaingloriously for the small triumph of showing thyself in the right and a wise man in the wrong; thou art not one whit the wiser therefor. Be not angry or unkind to anyone for trifles, lest thou make thyself enemies unnecessarily.

Do not refuse things out of mere obstinacy to thy fellow-citizens, rather put thy will below their wishes. Avoid, as much as may be, bad men, men of persistent angry feelings; thou canst get nothing from their company but shame. Be the first to extend courteous greeting to every one, whatever be his faith; provoke not to wrath one of another belief than thine.

3. *From* HAROKEACH

—ELEAZAR BEN JUDAH OF WORMS *(13th century)*

[123] No crown carries such royalty with it as doth humility; no monu-

ment gives such glory as an unsullied name; no worldly gain can equal that which comes from observing God's laws. The highest sacrifice is a broken and contrite heart; the highest wisdom is that which is found in the Law; the noblest of all ornaments is modesty; and the most beautiful of all things that man can do is to forgive wrong.

From the Jewish Moralists

Cherish a good heart when thou findest it in any one; hate, for thou mayest hate it, the haughtiness of the overbearing man, and keep the boaster at a distance. There is no skill or cleverness to be compared to that which avoids temptation; there is no force, no strength that can equal piey.

Let thy dealings be of such sort that a blush need never visit thy cheek; be sternly dumb to the voice of passion; commit no sin, saying to thyself that thou wilt repent and make atonement at a later time. Follow not the desire of the eyes, banish carefully all guile from thy soul, all unseemly self-assertion from thy bearing and thy temper.

Speak never mere empty words; enter into strife with no man; place no reliance on men of mocking lips; wrangle not with evil men; cherish no too fixed good opinion of thyself, but lend thine ear to remonstrance and reproof. Be not weakly pleased at demonstrations of honour; strive not anxiously for distinction; be never enviously jealous of others, or too eager for money.

Honour thy parents; make peace whenever thou canst among people, lead them gently into the good path; place thy trust in, give thy company to, those who fear God.

4. *From* HAROKEACH

—ELEAZAR BEN JUDAH OF WORMS *(13th century)*

If the means of thy support in life be measured out scantily to thee, remember that thou hast to be thankful and grateful even for the mere privilege to breathe, and that thou must take up that suffering as a test of thy piety and a preparation for better things. But if worldly wealth be lent to thee, exalt not thyself above thy· brother; for both of ye came naked into the world, and both of ye will surely have to sleep at last together in the dust.

From the Jewish Moralists

Bear well thy heart against the assaults of envy, which kills even sooner than death itself; and know no envy at all, save such envy of the merits of virtuous men as shall lead thee to emulate the beauty of their lives. Surrender not thyself a slave to hate, that ruin of all the heart's good resolves, that destroyer of the very savour of food, of our sleep, of all reverence in our souls.

Keep peace both within the city and without, for it goes well with all those who are counsellors of peace. Be wholly sincere; mislead no one by prevarications, by words smoother than intention, as little as by direct falsehood. For God the Eternal is a God of Truth; it is He from whom truth floweth first, He who begat truth and sent it into creation.

If thou hadst lived in the dread days of martyrdom, and the peoples had fallen on thee to force thee to apostatize from thy faith, thou wouldst surely, as did so many, have given thy life in its defence. Well then, fight now the fight laid on thee in the better days, the fight with evil desire; fight and conquer, and seek for allies in this warfare of your soul, seek them in the fear of God and the study of the Torah. Forget not that God recompenses according to the measure wherewith we withstand the evil in our heart. Be a man in thy youth; but if thou wert then defeated in the struggle, return, return at last to God, however old thou mayest be.

5. A FATHER'S ADMONITION

—MOSES MAIMONIDES *(11th century)*

Fear the Lord the God of thy Fathers and serve Him in love, for fear only restrains a man from sin, while love stimulates him to good. Accustom thyself to habitual goodness, for a man's character is what habit makes it.

If thou find in the Torah or the Prophets or the Sages a hard saying which thou canst not understand, stand fast by thy faith and attribute the fault to thine own want of intelligence. Place it in a corner of your heart for future consideration, but despise not thy Religion because thou art unable to understand one difficult matter.

Love truth and uprightness—the ornaments of the soul—and cleave unto them; prosperity so obtained is built on a sure rock. Keep firmly to thy word; let not a legal contract or witness be more binding than thine verbal promise, whether in public or in private. Disdain reservations and subterfuges, evasions and sharp practices. Woe to him who builds his house upon them. Abhor inactivity and indolence, the causes of bodily destruction of penury, of self-contempt—the ladders of Satan and his satellites. *From the Jewish Moralists*

Defile not your souls by quarrelsomeness and petulance. I have seen the white become black, the low brought still lower, families driven into exile, princes deposed from their high estate, great cities laid in ruins, assemblies dispersed, the pious humiliated, the honourable held lightly and despised, all on account of quarrelsomeness. Glory in forbearance, for in that is true strength and victory.

6. *From* SEFER CHASSIDIM

—JUDAH THE PIOUS *(13th century)*

Mislead no one through thy actions designedly, be he Jew or non-Jew. Injustice must be done to none, whether he belong to our Religion or to another.

If thou seest a strange man of another faith about to commit sin, prevent its coming to pass if it be in thy power, and herein let the prophet Jonah be thy model.

No blessing rests on the money of people who clip coin, make a practice of usury, use false weights and measures, and are in general not honest in business; their children lose their homes at last, and have to beg for bread.

Worthy of punishment is he, too, who heaps excessive burdens

on the carrying beasts, beats and tortures it; a sick or breeding beast·
should be tenderly dealt with.

When thou findest thyself among people who jeer and gibe,
leave them as quickly as thou canst; for mockery leads to want of
respect for one's self and others, and that is the high road to an
unchaste life.

Parents must on no account whatever, strike a grown-up son,
curse him, or so move him to wrath that he forget himself, and with
whom he is dealing.

On the Day of the Judgment, those who are of kindred virtue
and merit will find themselves in lasting companionship with each
other. The father then ceases to mourn and grieve over the son that
had left him; for the ineffable delight felt in the radiance of God's
countenance will send into oblivion all the anguish of earthly life.

7. *From* HAROKEACH

—ELEAZAR BEN JUDAH OF WORMS *(13th century)*

My son, wholly incompatible with a humble spirit is loud and passionate talk, falsehood, uttering of oaths, mockery, unrestrained
desire, vengefulness.

Cease to exalt thyself in thine own estimation, and let none of
thy failings appear small or trifling in thine own eyes, but all of
them weighty and great.

Keep far from all unseemly things; close thine eyes, thy ears to
them with stern decision; for there be desires which cause the soul
to be apostate from God. Therefore, in the days when thou art still
young, think of the Heavenly Father who created thee, supported
thee, clothed thee; and requite Him not, ungrateful, by delivering
up thy soul to impurity.

Remain faithful to the Torah; deny thyself even many things
that are permitted; be, so far as thou canst, ever of cheerful and
joyous temper; and forget not that it is to God, God Eternal, God
the Only One, to whom thy soul returns in death.

8. *From* SEMAG

—MOSES OF COUCY (*13th century*)

Those who lie freely to non-Jews and steal from them, are worse
than ordinary criminals. They are blasphemers; for it is due to their
guilt, that some say, "Jews have no binding law, no moral stand-
ards."

He who is but a novice in the fear of God will do well to say
audibly each day, as he rises:

"This day will I be a faithful servant of the Almighty; be on my
guard against wrath, falsehood, hatred, quarrelsomeness; will look
not too closely at women, and forgive those who wound me." For
whoso forgives is forgiven in turn. Hardheartedness and a temper
that will not make up quarrels, are a heavy burden of sin, unworthy
of an Isralite.

9. *From* THE WAY OF THE RIGHTEOUS

—A BOOK OF MORALS (*15th century*)

The thread on which the different good qualities of human beings
are strung as pearls, is the fear of God. When the fastenings of this
fear are unloosed, the pearls roll in all directions, and are lost one
by one. Even a single grave moral fault may be the ruin of all
other advantages; as when, for example, one is always setting off
his own excellence by bringing into prominence his neighbour's failings. Never put in words anything which can call up a blush on thine
own cheek or make another's grow pale.

Be not blind, but open-eyed to the great wonders of Nature,
familiar, everyday objects though they be to thee. But men are
more wont to be astonished at the sun's eclipse than at his unfail-
ing rise.

The aim of all thought, the highest of all merits, is love of God.
In comparison with the raptures of that love, all other delights
pale, even those we have in our children. The soul reaches the en-
chantments of this joy, is destined to enter into the appointed Place
where life grows and shines with a fire that shall never be quenched.

*From the
Jewish
Moralists*

[128]